Deferring Democracy

Deferring Democracy

Promoting Openness in Authoritarian Regimes

CATHARIN E. DALPINO

BROOKINGS INSTITUTION PRESS
Washington, D.C.

Copyright © 2000
THE BROOKINGS INSTITUTION
1775 Massachusetts Avenue, N.W., Washington, D.C. 20036
www.brookings.edu

Library of Congress Cataloging-in-Publication Data

Dalpino, Catharin E.
  Deferring democracy : promoting openness in authoritarian regimes /
Catharin E. Dalpino.
    p.   cm.
Includes bibliographical references and index.
  ISBN 0-8157-1701-6
  1. United States—Foreign relations—1989–. 2. World politics—1989–.
3. Authoritarianism. 4. Democratization. 5. Political development.
6. Social movements. I. Title.
E840 .D34 2000   00-009930
327.73—dc21   CIP
                        9 8 7 6 5 4 3 2 1

The paper used in this publication meets minimum requirements of the American
National Standard for Information Sciences—Permanence of Paper for Printed
Library Materials: ANSI Z39.48-1984.

Typeset in Minion

Composition by Circle Graphics,
Columbia, Md.

Printed by R. R. Donnelley and Sons,
Harrisonburg, Va.

₿ THE BROOKINGS INSTITUTION

The Brookings Institution is an independent organization devoted to nonpartisan research, education, and publication in economics, government, foreign policy, and the social sciences generally. Its principal purposes are to aid in the development of sound public policies and to promote public understanding of issues of national importance.

The Institution was founded on December 8, 1927, to merge the activities of the Institute for Government Research, founded in 1916, the Institute of Economics, founded in 1922, and the Robert Brookings Graduate School of Economics and Government, founded in 1924.

The general administration of the Institution is the responsibility of a Board of Trustees charged with safeguarding the independence of the staff and fostering the most favorable conditions for scientific research and publication. The immediate direction of the policies, program, and staff is vested in the president, assisted by an advisory committee of the officers and staff.

In publishing a study, the Institution presents it as a competent treatment of a subject worthy of public consideration. The interpretations or conclusions in such publications are those of the author or authors and do not necessarily reflect the views of the other staff members, officers, or trustees of the Brookings Institution.

To Teddy,

and to the memory of A. Doak Barnett,
Brookings Senior Fellow, 1969–82

Foreword

The democratic revolution that marked the end of the cold war was an incomplete one. It broke the communist monopoly in the Soviet Union and Eastern Europe and leavened authoritarianism with democratic experiments in several countries of Latin America, Africa, and Asia. However, fully one-third of the world's people still live under repressive government, with regimes that refuse to oblige cold war triumphalists with easy ideological victories. Defined by their lack of formal democracy and their questionable human rights practices, these countries are broadly viewed as political intransigents, out of step with post–cold war democratic values.

Yet in a number of key countries authoritarianism is softening, and cautious new political experiments are underway. Although Leninism lingers in China, the regime there has commenced market and other economic reforms. The resulting political dislocation has brought unexpected (and unannounced) civil and political freedoms that fall short of a democratic transition but nevertheless represent an improvement in the daily lives of citizens. In years to come, Vietnam may follow a similar path. In Iran, the nature of the Islamic republic is under review, not only by the broader population but also by the country's ruling clergy. Within the structure of political Islam, reforms are being promoted that permit greater popular participation and voice. In the traditional monarchies of the Middle East, a new generation of leaders is assuming power and demonstrating a more pragmatic approach to government, which may offer opportunities for enlarging the political space and protecting rights.

Catharin Dalpino examines these important and puzzling countries with an eye to entry points for external actors to encourage greater political openness. In doing so, she measures present U.S. policy against the realities in these countries and in light of emerging social and political trends. She questions whether the example of the collapse of the Soviet system is applicable to the more evolutionary pace of change in these countries, particularly in view of the mixed results on political and economic reform seen in Russia. On the operational side, Dalpino questions whether the cold war instruments applied by some U.S. policymakers are effective in encouraging these regimes to loosen controls. Lastly, this book puts forward an alternative policy paradigm, arguing that in order to promote greater political freedoms in these countries, policymakers must paradoxically set aside their democracy framework in the near term.

The author is grateful for the support she received from numerous colleagues in researching and writing this book. In particular, she thanks Larry Diamond for his encouragement and David Steinberg for his thoughtful comments on the draft manuscript. Suzanne Maloney provided valuable insight and information on current Iranian political processes. The author is grateful to Minxin Pei and Nancy Yuan for their help in providing or obtaining primary data and sources. She thanks Richard Haass for his constructive comments and his Promethean patience during the drafting process, as well as Susan Jackson, Todd DeLelle, and Fabian Nierhaus for their verification work. Charles Dibble of the Brookings Press edited the book, Inge Lockwood proofread it, and Julia Petrakis provided the index.

The views expressed in this book are those of the author and should not be ascribed to the trustees, officers, or other staff members of the Brookings Institution.

MICHAEL H. ARMACOST
President

Washington, D.C.
September 2000

Contents

Deferring Democracy

1

Introduction

The peaceful democratic transitions in Eastern and Central Europe in the late 1980s and early 1990s were tailor-made for American sentiments. When the linchpin of Soviet domination was removed, postcommunist leaders in the region reflexively pledged their support for the principles of democracy and free markets. In contrast to the more gradual, sometimes indiscernible, movement toward democracy in other regions, the transitions in Eastern Europe had a decisive ring, punctuated by such dramatic moments as the fall of the Berlin Wall. And in the subsequent transformation of the geopolitical map—the "velvet divorce" of Czechoslovakia, the reunification of Germany, and the initial separation of the Yugoslav states—the automatic assumption was that any new state would also be democratic.

It is understandable that the West, and the United States in particular, would respond to this astonishing chain of events with euphoria and an unequivocal sense of triumph. Zero-sum struggles, as many perceived the ideological competition of the cold war to be, serve up more complete victories. Equally important, the return of the Eastern European states to genuine, rather than nominal, self-rule brought the cold war to a full-circle conclusion. In the battle that began over the capture of Eastern European populations by the Soviet Union and the imposition of communism upon them, cold war liberation theology appeared to have worked.

Mitigating factors are noted but often obscured. The liberation of Eastern Europe was launched by the Soviet Union itself, when President Mikhail

Gorbachev revoked the Brezhnev doctrine of hard-line (as opposed to reform) communism for the Eastern bloc. Nor did the sudden collapse of communism instantly produce its democratic opposite. In the southern tier of Eastern Europe, particularly the former Yugoslavia, new electoral democracies were shattered by ethnic conflict, often engineered by nationalist demagogues who had come to power through popular elections. Even the northern tier countries, some of which had democratic experience before communism, were forced to confront lingering authoritarian practices beneath the surface of their new democracies. One irony of the postcommunist period was the 1995 electoral defeat of Poland's president Lech Walesa, possibly the most renowned dissident of the 1980s, by the leader of a former communist faction.[1] But these qualifications notwithstanding, the seeming swiftness of the Eastern European transitions created a paradigm of democratic revolution for many in the U.S. foreign policy community and a prescription for democracy promotion in countries still under repressive rule.

Against this backdrop, several key countries have defied the democratic contagion, commonly known as the Third Wave, that has seemed to sweep through the former Soviet block and parts of Asia and Africa in the past twenty years.[2] As a result, political practices in these countries often draw an unusual degree of scrutiny and criticism in the U.S. policy community. Although negative views of these states persist, some are in the midst of reform efforts that are reshaping relations between state and society and that carry the possibility, but by no means the guarantee, of future democratization. These experiments are largely uncharted territory. Most of these societies have no democratic experience in living memory; at best, they may have had brief episodes of relative openness.

This study examines U.S. policy in those countries that are opening windows to political and social reform (often as a consequence of attempts at economic reform) but are still ranked among the most repressive in the world by Western standards. It focuses on states in which power rests in the hands of a collective authority or ideologically determined group, however much that ideology may have waned. Some are postrevolutionary societies, such as China, Vietnam, and Iran, whose current experiments in openness can be attributed both to the successes and the failures of their revolutions. Their regimes are distinct from those produced by strict personal rule, such as that of Ferdinand Marcos in the Philippines, Mobutu Sese Seko in Zaire, or Suharto in Indonesia. Because these regimes have been more successful than personalistic ones in institutionalizing rule, their control has endured beyond the first generation. Indeed, some of these states have undergone significant (if unheralded) transitions from one-man to corporatist rule and from totalitarianism to authoritarianism. Nevertheless, incumbents are determined to manage change in a manner that maintains continuity and a central role for the regime. These societies are in the process of gradual political liberalization but have not attempted a formal democratic transition. In that respect, they are different from many semiauthoritarian countries in which a democratic transition has stalled or failed.

Present U.S. policy to promote political change in these countries does not recognize nor does it reinforce these positive trends and ultimately does not serve U.S. interests. By advocating—indeed, often insisting upon—immediate democratization and the guarantee of human rights in societies where political change is a complex and volatile process, the United States is often viewed as ideologically self-serving and overly simplistic, even reckless, by reformers and hard-liners alike in these countries. At the least, these strident and unrealistic policies can raise nationalist hackles (and anti-Americanism) in the broader population of the target country and marginalize U.S. influence on domestic processes. At worst, they can exacerbate the instability that is inherent in political and social change by upsetting delicate internal dynamics.

This study proposes a policy to promote openness in these countries that builds upon existing trends of liberalization and that need not wait until a democratic transition is in sight. The underlying thesis of this policy is that the best way to promote liberalization in these countries and build a more solid foundation for an eventual transition to democracy is to defer a democracy promotion effort for the near term. Whether or not liberalization becomes a stepping stone to democratization, a successful policy will produce a net gain for political pluralism and the protection of rights.

An effective policy to promote liberalization requires an understanding of the differences between the processes of liberalization and democratization, terms that are broadly and loosely applied in the academic and policy communities. For the purpose of this study, liberalization is defined as a loosening of control by an authoritarian regime without the intention to move immediately toward a democratic transition. Authoritarian leaders most often relax or modify their own rules in an attempt to preserve the core of their power because their legitimacy or their performance has come under widespread domestic criticism. Whatever freedoms this may bring, the underlying goal of the regime is to strengthen public support for its rule.

In the course of liberalization, some individual and group rights may be extended, and these improvements may even be codified in the legal system. However, dramatic institutional reform that guarantees the widespread protection of citizens' rights and enshrines popular selection and control over leaders must usually await democratization.[3] In this regard, democratization can be viewed in terms of institutional transformation, among other functions. Liberalization is best conceived as a process of transforming relationships—among members of the regime, between the regime and state, the state and society, the people and their rulers, and even among everyday citizens—that stops short of comprehensive institutional reform. Because it emanates from the regime itself, liberalization can be unannounced and halting, while democratization is a more deliberate and public process, requiring the involvement of a wider range of political and social actors.

Democratization is usually preceded by liberalization, but democracy cannot be taken as the assured outcome of a liberal experiment. History has shown that such experiments are just as likely to produce systems suspended in "soft authoritarianism" for decades,[4] or cause a return to previous levels of repression. The uncertain nature of the liberalization process discourages the notion of a brisk and seamless sequence with a political democracy as the immediate goal.

In light of these risks, in many of the countries in this study a policy to promote liberalization rather than democratization is arguably the better path at this time. Realistically, the hold maintained by these regimes often makes liberalization the only viable option. Moreover, the gradual nature and incremental pace of liberalization offers the possibility of combining some degree of stability with political change. Although "stability" is viewed by some as shorthand for maintaining the status quo, in volatile societies with social or ethnic cleavages that pose a risk of serious disruption, or in postrevolutionary societies with living memory of widespread political violence, it may be a requisite element of any process of political change.

In comparison to democratization, the signs of liberalization are more difficult to detect from the outside, and the processes of liberalization are less responsive to external intervention. Political liberalization can be an official policy; more often, it begins as the regime's tacit no-objection to openness created in other areas of reform. Either way, it is a high-risk undertaking. In the early stages of liberalization, progress is usually dependent upon maintaining the incumbent's sense of security. Political rules are in flux and are difficult to discern. When tacit boundaries are violated, the regime's actions can be swift and brutal, as was the case in Burma in 1988, when widespread prodemocracy demonstrations were suppressed, or in China in 1989, when the Tiananmen Square movement to urge reform of the regime was brought to a violent end. The result can be a net loss of personal and political freedom for a number of years. For opposite reasons, the uncertainty of the liberalization process creates nervousness among authoritarian rulers and would-be democrats alike. In this instance, these two groups are often, in the words of a Chinese proverb, "sleeping in the same bed but dreaming different dreams."[5]

Beyond the tenacity of their rulers, the authoritarian countries considered in this study have characteristics that call for an approach to political development different from that of the recent wave of democratic transitions. The remaining Leninist systems (all of which are in Asia, with the exception of Cuba) are rooted as much (or more) in authoritarian tradition and nationalism as in communist doctrine, making sudden collapse less likely than in the Soviet bloc. Another set of nations, primarily in the Middle East, have Muslim-majority populations facing strong Islamic fundamentalist pressure.[6] Abrupt political change in these countries, even movement toward democracy, could either cause an authoritarian backlash from regime conservatives or create an opening to an Islamic fundamentalist order.[7]

U.S. policy tends to ignore immediate opportunities for promoting beneficial changes in these societies and, as a result, pushes our own goals farther from our grasp. In policy toward the remaining Leninist states, particularly China, this can be attributed in part to lingering cold war views that press for rapid democratization—even an authoritarian collapse in the Eastern European mode—and rely upon outdated cold war practices. A different dynamic applies to U.S. Middle East policy, which is largely influenced by security concerns—over access to oil, the Arab-Israeli peace process, and the nature and intentions of political Islam[8]–that temper enthusiasm for political change in the policy community.[9] Democracy promotion has nevertheless filtered into U.S. assistance programs for the region, as evidenced by the inauguration in 1997 of the Middle East Democracy Fund, which allocates money for small projects administered by the State Department.

With both the Asian Leninist regimes and the Middle Eastern states, appropriate strategies are lacking because democracy promotion is perceived as negating broader bilateral and regional policy goals and because conditions in these countries do not meet the criteria for impending democratization. This study advocates a policy to promote openness in these systems while deferring pressure to democratize, a policy more consonant with other U.S. policy goals and likely to be more effective in encouraging political change.

In pursuit of such policy, this study looks first at reforms of state and society in a sample of liberalizing countries of particular concern to the United States. On the basis of reforming trends in these countries, an alternative model for U.S. policy is proposed, with recommendations for change in paradigms and practices. At present, the most significant target of opportunity is China, because of its current trends, its present and potential role in the international community, and its near-normal relations with the United States. In comparison to Vietnam and Laos (and particularly to the still-Stalinist North Korea), China is by far the most liberalizing of the Asian Leninist states,[10] despite the regime's continued crackdown on groups that are perceived to threaten the ruling order. These presently range from a small would-be political opposition, the China Democracy Party, to the much larger and apparently apolitical Falun Gong.

Key liberalizing regimes in the Middle East, the most important of which is Iran, are also considered. In comparison to several other Middle Eastern states, Iran has a high degree of political openness, all the more significant because it has evolved under an Islamic regime. However, U.S. relations with Iran are dramatically less developed than U.S.-China relations, leaving the United States with fewer openings to encourage political reform. Signs of liberalization are also emerging in some traditional monarchies of the Middle East, albeit at a slower and more cautious pace.

At any given point, the recommendations in this study may be immediately useful in only a few countries. They apply in full to China at the present time but would be difficult for the United States to implement in Iran. Some recommendations presently pertain to the Leninist states of Southeast Asia but are likely to have little effect on draconian totalitarian states such as North Korea. They may form the basis for policy to promote liberalization in Burma when the beginning of an attitudinal shift or a widening spectrum is seen within the military regime.[11] In the Gulf States under traditional rule, these policy prescriptions best apply to Kuwait, which has continued the liberalization experiment it began after the Gulf War. They are likely to have some use but not the fullest possible impact at this time on more entrenched traditional regimes, such as that of Saudi Arabia.

It is not the intention of this study to suggest that those countries that appear to be sitting out the Third Wave of democratization are in any way monolithic. Assembly-line policy has proved to be ineffective with the present democratizing systems, even among those emerging from a common political bloc.[12] Although some broad similarities may be found, easy equations are deceptive, even dangerous, for this new group of liberalizing regimes because of significant differences in political structures and history and because of deeply rooted indigenous forces. For example, it would be inaccurate to equate modernization automatically with democratization in either Iran or China. Many democratic transitions during the 1980s occurred in countries that had reached certain standards of economic development and social mobility.[13] To date, however, both China and Iran have demonstrated some ability to raise the standard of living of their citizens and to allow some access to modern features such as global media without significant impact on their political systems.

At the same time, it would be incorrect to assume that modernization presents identical attractions and problems in each society. It is generally seen as a positive force in China, while its long-standing equation with Western values makes it a double-edged sword in Iran. Neither do the regimes in this study necessarily pursue reforms with equal vigor. Iran's experiment in political liberalization is presently more extensive than those of the Asian Leninist regimes. However, Beijing and Hanoi are currently more invested in market reform than Teheran.

Rather, the regimes in this study are bound by a common paradox. They are more entrenched than authoritarian rulers in many other states. Asian Leninist regimes, Islamist governments, and traditional monarchies are inherently more conservative and (by virtue of history, tradition, or revolutionary claim) more embedded in the political and social fabric than many of the regimes that crumbled after the cold war. On the other hand, several of these states are undergoing a process of change more dynamic than that found in seemingly more benign regimes whose liberal reforms have long since stopped.

An Optimistic Paradigm and a Cautionary Tale

For most of the 1990s, Americans favored a model of political change that, in mythology if not in experience, sidesteps the disturbing ambiguities of the liberalization process and obviates the need to deal with questionable ruling elites. The events in Eastern Europe in 1989 had resonance with Americans not only because they seemed to deliver a clear-cut ideological victory, but because they also reinforced a model of "people power" revolution that had been building in the 1980s. The popular version of this model features mass demonstrations or strikes that force the collapse of an authoritarian regime, to be replaced immediately by democratic government. Through this lens, every popular demonstration is a potential democratic uprising, and every attempt to suppress a demonstration is an effort to stem a democratic revolution. The Chinese government's crackdown on demonstrators in Tiananmen Square in 1989 is remembered in some American policy circles more for what might have been than for the actual event.

The genesis of this paradigm in contemporary American thinking is the example of the Philippines, a close ally of the United States, in 1986. Three days of popular demonstrations in Manila led by the National Movement for Free Elections (NAMFREL) not only mobilized popular resistance to Ferdinand Marcos but also caused two key military leaders to break from the regime and provide crucial support to Corazon Aquino. The outcome vindicated a last-minute decision by the Reagan administration to abandon support for Marcos and provided some balance to U.S. cold war policy in the Philippines, in which concern for maintaining security had helped Marcos accumulate authoritarian powers.[14] Public demonstrations in Eastern Europe later in the decade were accorded similar weight, although accounts of that time point to decisions made in Moscow to disengage from the Soviet satellites preceding disturbances on the ground. In reality, the only genuine "people power" revolution in Eastern Europe occurred in Romania, although mass mobilization clearly strengthened the hand of reformers in Poland and Czechoslovakia.

This paradigm is even less common in the broader spectrum of countries outside Eastern Europe that have begun transitions to democracy in the past twenty years. Apart from the Philippines, only Portugal and Greece (and to a lesser extent Indonesia) have followed the path of "people power" revolution. The great majority of transitions have involved complex negotiations between authoritarian regimes and opposition groups, with substantially longer time frames. Preparing the ground for these negotiations in advance of any tangible signs of democratization often involved years of gradual liberalization, in which the regime debated political reform while civil society was reorganized and reoriented. Even most "collapse" countries underwent some preliminary period of liberalization. In the Philippines, NAMFREL's successful maneuvers were the culmination of a process originating in the mid-1970s, when Marcos began to loosen martial law and civil groups worked to widen political space.

The assumption of a popular groundswell behind every transition to democracy has encouraged the view of democracy as a universal aspiration. By extension, all populations in authoritarian societies are pressing constantly and restively for democracy, and therefore all authoritarian states are or should be on the verge of democratic transitions.[15] Promoting democracy universally is accordingly a logical policy goal.[16] Despite the difficulties that some new democracies have faced in consolidating their systems, and even the reappearance of authoritarian trends,[17] belief in a democratic trajectory remains strong.

Some Americans renewed this belief in observance of the tenth anniversary of the fall of the Berlin Wall, but a more mixed celebration approaches, marking a decade after the collapse of the Soviet Union. The democratic victory that is widely held to have occurred at the cold war's end invariably includes the dissolution of the Soviet Union and attempts by some of the national governments to move toward democracy. The most important of these is clearly Russia. In reality, however, the Russian experience of the 1980s and 1990s runs counter to the tenets of the Berlin Wall paradigm. The "second Russian revolution," as analysts now frame those decades, was distinguished by its lack of major protest movements.[18] Russian dissidents whose names appeared on the lists compiled by concerned American human rights officials in the 1970s and 1980s did not lead the charge for reform, nor did they emerge in prominent positions in the new democratic government. Rather, the push for change came from the "partocracy"—Mikhail Gorbachev, Edward Shevardnadze, and Boris Yeltsin—all of whom had held positions in the inner circle of Brezhnev's ruling structure.[19] Indeed, the public apathy toward reform in the 1980s hampered Gorbachev's efforts, because it weakened his ability to override the resistance of hard-line party officials. Yeltsin's more vocal (if erratic) attempts to generate popular support were enough to maintain an electoral edge but not enough to mobilize widespread public consensus for his reforms.

But Russia did follow the Berlin Wall model in the swift collapse of old institutions. The ensuing years have revealed the difficulties of a rapid exit from authoritarianism and central planning when foundations had not been laid for more democratic institutions, much less for the legal and administrative infrastructure needed for open markets. Without traction in these areas, Russia lurched from one crisis to another for most of the decade: the attempted coup of 1991, the political violence brought on by warring factions in 1993, and the economic meltdown of 1998. On another track, the sudden collapse of Soviet sovereignty and the need to refashion a Russian national ethic in short order gave rise to the Chechnyan uprising and a severe response from the central government. The collective weight of these problems has helped to usher in a new president, Vladimir Putin, who has vowed to alleviate social misery, hoist the Russian economy, and banish political gloom through a "dictatorship of law,"[20] a slogan that inspires both hope and fear in Russia's democratic quarter.

Power in Russia has yet to be rebalanced between the executive and the legislature; as a result, executive power is still predominant, if more democratically inclined, and vulnerable to one-man rule. Some realists might consider this to be for the better at this time, since the communists remain the largest political party in the Duma, although their influence may well have waned with the 1999 election. Beyond political standoffs, a more insidious trend threatens to overtake the Russian political system. The uncertainties of political and economic reform since the Soviet Union's collapse have given a boost to new economic oligarchies, whose rapid accumulation of power seems impervious to the meager checks and balances presently available.[21] This, in turn, has helped elevate political and economic corruption to near-ruinous levels, a trend exacerbated by the rise of organized criminal groups.[22] This unfortunate trajectory is testimony to the weakness of the Russian legal system and to the lack of a widespread supporting belief in the rule of law.

There is little the United States can do to help Russian reformers reverse these trends in the short term, although it should clearly continue to promote economic and political reform wherever possible. Nor should Americans give way to total despair over Russia's political future. Administration officials are correct in pointing out that organized repression of individual rights in Russia is gone; despite coup attempts and other upsets, Russia has not abandoned its quest for a democratic order.[23] With several elections behind it, Russia seems to have settled into a democratic form, if the content is often lacking.

There are, however, lessons to be learned from the Russian example for U.S. policy toward authoritarian states. First is the recognition that, contrary to the popular post–cold war paradigm, reform may at times originate from the attitudes of elites rather than the desperate maneuvers of freedom-deprived masses. A related point is that the public may lag behind, rather than lead, demands for political change. A final and important lesson is that complicated political, economic, and legal systems do not spring up spontaneously; they are doubly difficult to create in the void left by a collapsed system. A more incremental process of change, if not as romantic as the collapse scenario, is likely to be more successful, and it may be shorter in the end. The Russian case suggests that a very rapid democratic transition can turn into a very protracted one.

The Democratic Imperative

If the paradigms driving U.S. policy after the cold war make it difficult to imagine regimes that are not on a democratic fast-track, the policy apparatus makes it difficult to deal with such states. Democracy promotion has been an explicit goal in U.S. policy since the onset of the cold war, but it has changed dramatically in form and focus since that time.

In the early years of the cold war, a simple bipolar view of regimes as either communist or noncommunist caused political support and economic assistance to be focused on anticommunist allies, actual or potential. However, ideological competition in the newly decolonized Third World proved stronger than originally anticipated. U.S. strategies frequently combined aid with efforts to persuade populations of the advantages of democracy. Communist regimes were naturally targeted for public condemnation. Moral support to populations behind the Iron Curtain in Eastern Europe and the Bamboo Curtain in Asia was considered essential. As a practical matter, however, there was little that could be done directly, other than broadcasts that attempted to counter government propaganda. Despite occasional periods of political thaw, U.S. democracy promotion policy toward the Eastern bloc was essentially symbolic until the late 1980s.

A more nuanced approach developed toward dictatorship from the right. By the late 1950s, the authoritarian excesses of some anticommunist allies had become an embarrassment for the United States, domestically as well as abroad. A more calibrated view of the political spectrum was emerging, one that acknowledged that anticommunism did not always yield democracy. This realization often sent American policymakers on a quixotic search for a "third force" in developing countries—democratically minded leaders with popular support who were strong enough to fend off insurgencies from the left and coup attempts from the right.[24] Finding few such leaders, by the 1980s the United States had settled upon a two-pronged approach to promoting democracy among its allies: diplomatic pressure urging regimes to curb the most egregious abuses,[25] and political assistance programs to strengthen democratic institutions, primarily in Latin America.[26]

During the last decade of the cold war, American democracy promotion aimed at the Eastern bloc became slightly more dimensional as well. Reform efforts in Eastern Europe created the minimum of political space needed for the emergence of civil society organizations. These groups, the most prominent of which was the Solidarity labor movement in Poland, sought openly to challenge the state. The phenomenon of these organizations was twofold: they were able to function as surrogate political oppositions, and they were able to establish links with civil society groups in the West. Overt U.S. assistance in this effort was managed primarily through private American organizations, such as the National Endowment for Democracy,[27] using public funds. The political character of this assistance and the practice of supporting a nascent but defiant civil society while maintaining pressure on the government had strong appeal for many anticommunist warriors.

Although modest democracy initiatives were launched sporadically in a number of regions, the United States did not have a global strategy apart from anticommunism to promote democracy during the cold war era. In the post–cold war environment, however, a universal approach seemed natural to many Americans because of the range of new democratic transitions and the growing tendency to view economic, social, and political issues in transnational terms. By the 1970s, with the rise of multinational corporations and economic cartels, the concept of an increasingly interdependent world economy had entered popular consciousness. During the late 1980s and early 1990s, with authoritarian regimes appearing to fall in domino fashion, the notion of a worldwide political demonstration effect was taking hold. In the official policy community this translated into bureaucratic reforms made within foreign affairs agencies. Governments, and bureaucracies in particular, tend to act as bellwethers; by 1993 high-ranking positions to oversee global affairs (some specifically tagged for democracy) had been created in the National Security Council, the Department of State, the United States Agency for International Development, and the intelligence agencies. The position of assistant secretary of defense for democracy and peacekeeping was also proposed by the administration but ultimately was not approved by Congress.

The full impact of this shift was most readily seen in official assistance programs. A universal approach not only reconfigured democracy assistance within the U.S. government but altered the very definition of foreign aid. In the early 1990s, funding for democracy promotion increased dramatically. Statistics on democracy assistance had not been maintained under a discrete category until then, but unofficial inventories estimate that such assistance seldom exceeded $100 million per year before 1989. By 1991 assistance under a broad definition of democracy promotion had climbed to $682 million and by 1993 to $900 million.[28] By that time, major assistance packages for support of democracy in Eastern Europe and the former Soviet Union had been legislated,[29] and initiatives were quickly assembled for several other regions.[30] A global approach also required that common denominators for successful programs be established, which were quickly translated into common indicators for progress in democratization itself.

These indicators tend to adopt concrete measurements, similar to those employed for economic development and infrastructure projects, with an emphasis on quantifiable outputs: the percentage of voters who turn out on election day, the number of judges trained, the volume of bills considered by new democratic legislatures.[31] Progress is assumed when the numbers go up. However, these instruments are seldom useful for gauging the will to reform, in either ruling circles or civil society groups, and so they measure half the progress at best. Moreover, they are designed to assess positive political change but are weak in detecting the warning signs that could send democratization into reverse or in tracking a process that is seldom linear.

Beyond altering the size and shape of democracy assistance programs, post–cold war policy has injected democratization into the criteria for aid allocation. Under the "sustainable development" formula of the U.S. Agency for International Development, a country's eligibility for assistance is judged according to a basket of conditions, one of which is the recipient government's progress toward democratization or its intention to democratize (often measured by movement toward a transitional election).[32] Although the interpretation of an acceptable threshold of democratization often varies from one country to another, this approach to assistance reverses the cold war dynamic: rather than offering aid to induce movement toward democracy, assistance now assumes that movement.[33]

This practice has been buttressed in Congress by a series of amendments to the 1961 Foreign Assistance Act, as well as other legislative initiatives, that attempt to set acceptable levels of political development for aid recipients. The majority of these are ad hoc initiatives aimed at specific countries. In addition, automatic mechanisms are intended to prevent governments that perpetrate gross violations of human rights from receiving assistance and cut off aid to regimes that overthrow elected governments by force. Although some of these measures trace their origins to human rights policy of the 1970s and do not mandate democracy per se, they prescribe a level of freedom that is usually found only in liberal democracies.

Like most automatic sanctions, however, these provisions have built-in problems for implementation. The prohibition of aid to gross human rights abusers might appear to be a self-evident strategy for any human rights policy. In practice, however, human rights officials in the executive branch resist implementing this amendment because of the lack of a shared definition of gross abuse. In addition, a government whose level of abuse is only slightly below the cut-off point may be seen as exempt from pressure or reprisal. A second condition, commonly known as the military coup clause because it addresses the violent overthrow of an elected government, is more frequently implemented. However, it is difficult to apply to violations within the ruling structure, where many problems originate. This was the case with the "auto-coup" of President Alberto Fujimori in Peru against his own government, and the events of July 1997 in Cambodia, when Second Prime Minister Hun Sen drove his senior partner Prince Ranariddh out of the ruling coalition with a show of force. Moreover, as sanctions proliferate in U.S. foreign policy, states with questionable political practices—nuclear proliferation, state-sponsored terrorism, or failure to cooperate on narcotics interdiction—may already have had their assistance reduced or removed under other laws. In

1999 the military coup clause was moot in the face of a military takeover in Pakistan because aid was already prohibited under the Pressler and Glenn amendments, both of which address nuclear weapons issues.

Apart from democracy's place in the foundation of post–cold war assistance, it has featured increasingly in international negotiations to resolve internal conflicts, often through the mechanism of a transitional election. Increasingly, these elections are managed by the international community. Because there is usually profound deterioration in the political, social, and even physical infrastructure by the time the conflict is resolved, large and comprehensive assistance packages are usually required during the post-election period. Democratization figures heavily in these packages. In the 1990s, a number of postconflict states—Cambodia, Haiti, Bosnia, Liberia, and East Timor—were ministered by the international community in this way, with significant contributions from the United States.[34]

Handling "Intransigent" Hold-Outs

The approach to nondemocratic states in this new framework also underscores the assumption of a universal democratic movement. Authoritarian governments are usually chastised for their intransigence in the face of global democratization. In assistance programs, however, they are labeled as "pretransition" or "prebreakthrough" states, categorically assuming a democratization process, however distant.[35] Ruling elites in these states are assumed to be the primary obstacle to democratic change. Accordingly, attention is focused upon alternative groups that are judged to be the future engines of a democratic transition. Available measures are employed to provide support, even safe haven, for these embattled opposition groups or for what is assumed to be an opposition.

In most of the countries that form the central focus of this study, the "pretransition" approach to promoting political change is implausible at this point. In the liberalizing Asian Leninist states, no organized political opposition has emerged (or, at this stage, can emerge) to provide a beachhead for external support. Nor has a critical mass of advocacy organizations formed to function as a surrogate political opposition. The Middle East presents additional complications. In some systems, even those in which a formal opposition is permitted to operate to any degree, citizen-state relations and basic definitions of political legitimacy depart from standard Western models. In the past, the intelligentsia in some societies were the major champions of socialist and nationalist reforms and were viewed as having endorsed authoritarian practices as a result.[36] More recently, the increased role of religion in political and social affairs, ranging from Muslim-based social service groups to Islamist political factions, raises questions about the ability of civil society in these countries to deliver a democratic political opposition as it is understood in the West.

Although internal dynamics ultimately determine the prospects for political change, they are only one of the challenges facing U.S. policy to promote democracy in these countries. Policy trade-offs are particularly difficult with many of these states. Some hold strategic advantages because of their role in regional negotiations (China with respect to the Four Party talks on North Korea, Jordan in the Middle East peace process) or because of their vital resources (Saudi Arabia, Kuwait). Some (such as China) are calculated to become future economic powers and key trading partners. Some are also perceived as presenting strategic threats, which include concerns about terrorism and nuclear proliferation, and are subject to containment strategies as a result (Iran and, for some, China).

Those countries with large and heterogeneous populations (ethnically or regionally) pose a potential security threat of increasing concern in the post–cold war world—that of violent internal conflict. Humanitarian concerns aside, the international community might be able to tolerate a "failed" Haiti of 7 million people. It could not risk a "failed" China of 1.3 billion. At worst, the resulting chaos from a collapsing China would have a profound effect on the stability of Asia, and on U.S. policy to guarantee the security of its Asian allies. At the least, China could turn to the West for economic relief and reconstruction, the pricetag of which would be overwhelming.

Such factors underscore the need for caution in attempting to influence the internal political affairs of these nations in order to avoid disturbing fragile, circumstantial alliances or exacerbating tensions. Internally, they argue for a sound process of political change without dramatic disruption or the risk of violent reversal.

These important but ambiguous relations are further complicated in some cases by the absence of full normalization. As a result, access and leverage are restricted, sometimes severely so. Relations with the Asian Leninist states vary in their degree of normalization, but no relationship can be said to be fully secure. Of these, the most advanced is with China, but annual debates in Congress over most favored nation status during the 1990s and the pitched debate over permanent normal trade relations for China during the year 2000 are reminders that the relationship has not reached reliable equilibrium. Diplomatic recognition was recently achieved with Vietnam, but trade relations are not yet fully normalized. At present, official relations of any kind with Iran are nonexistent. President Muhammad Khatami has called for improved relations, but he has been careful to confine them to unofficial exchanges that are unlikely to fuel anti-American sentiment or threaten support for his reforms. To date, he has rejected the proposal for an American interests section in Teheran, the first formal step toward the normalization of official relations.

Normalization with these countries is hampered by historic antagonisms that resonate in domestic populations on both sides. In relations with Iran, the events of the late 1970s, when the dying shah was granted entry into the United States and American embassy officials were seized as hostages in Teheran, still cast a shadow. Indeed, many analysts consider the clergy's public support of the hostage-taking to have tipped the scales in favor of fundamentalist rule in Iran.[37] It was doubtless a defining event in the American political psyche, which continues to view Islamic government as invariably repressive and anti-American. The communist victory over South Vietnam and issues over American prisoners of war have cast long shadows over U.S.-Vietnamese relations. In the United States, such transitional events generated hostility not only toward the governments of these nations but also among Americans themselves. For the last half-century, disagreements have lingered over who "lost" China in 1949 (an issue that ushered in the McCarthy era), whose decisions ultimately led to the fall of Saigon in 1975, and who failed to commission (or read) the "right" intelligence on Iran in 1979. These dynamics are changing, particularly as prominent victims in these cases have encouraged Washington to pursue new paths with old adversaries.[38] Nevertheless, nationalist hackles are easily raised on both sides, and attempts to influence political development in these societies can invite suspicion that old agendas are in play.

Nor are these suspicions confined to old guard ideologues who waged anti-Western campaigns decades ago. Demographic change is sure to moderate resentment over past conflicts with the United States. Roughly half the population of Vietnam was born after 1975 and demonstrates little awareness or appreciation for the revolutionary changes of their parents' generation. The

post-1979 population explosion in Iran, urged by the ruling clerics, has produced a baby boom that, ironically, is more amenable to increased contact
with the United States and other Western societies. However, these changes
do not prevent bouts of nationalism, often urged by regimes to deflect attention from economic policy failures. Nationalism is promoted by some regimes
as a substitute for ideology after the cold war.[39] It is also seen in countries with
new economic power (and prestige) resulting from rapid growth, even among
the newly minted professional and middle classes. This nationalist resurgence
can be confusing to some Western promoters of democracy when they dis-
cover that their efforts are suspect in the liberal communities of a target society. Many Americans were surprised when Chinese students, who had been
the standard-bearers in Tiananmen Square in 1989, probed for the "hidden
agenda" behind U.S. human rights policy during President Clinton's address
to Peking University in 1998.[40] Nor is this phenomenon restricted to authoritarian countries. Since the end of the cold war, some democratizing societies
have found that nationalism is revived as democratic ideals are strengthened.
In the post-Marcos Philippines, for example, the democratically elected Sen-
ate voted not to renew the agreement for U.S. bases.

As these societies move along an uncertain path, nationalism also provides
insurance for the regime against the threats posed by external influence.
Under siege domestically, regimes see nationalism as a sealant, helping to
keep discussion (and disagreement) within national borders. Reform efforts
in these states are an undeniable acknowledgment by the ruling order that
many of the structures they had installed and maintained are seriously flawed
or no longer viable. China's per capita income at the end of the Cultural
Revolution, for example, was one of the lowest in the world, roughly on par
with that of Somalia.[41] This led to the reform platform introduced by Deng
Xiaoping; by the late 1980s, however, it was increasingly clear to the Chinese
population that Deng's economic measures were not adequately supported
by political reform. The system could not accommodate new constituencies
created by economic reform, nor curb rising corruption and inflation. In
Vietnam, the Communist Party turned to *doi moi* ("new thinking") in 1986
to pull the country out of severe economic distress, the result of a decade of
central planning and the costs of military occupation in Cambodia.

In Iran, failed economic policies in the postrevolutionary decade, a drop in
oil prices, and the drain of the Iran-Iraq War created serious social unrest in
the early 1990s. Attempts by President Ali Akbar Hashemi-Rafsanjani to ini-

tiate economic reforms on the margins of strict clerical control were largely unsuccessful.[42] The election of Mohammad Khatami in 1997, with 70 percent of the popular vote, was a watershed because his platform of political liberalization gave a referendum quality to the election. The 2000 parliamentary elections could further strengthen the mandate for economic reform. Assuming it is allowed to go forward, the new reform-dominated parliament may lend more support to Khatami's economic initiatives than its predecessor parliaments, which were captive to conservative interests.[43]

In many Middle Eastern states under traditional rule, regime legitimacy has come under scrutiny because of the revenue crisis of the late 1980s when, as in Iran, declining oil prices caused a drop in these countries' gross national product. These fiscal declines encouraged debate over resource allocation and economic policy. More important, in many cases they forced the state to curtail government funding in several sectors. Economic functions were moved to the private sector, and civil society became more involved in education and welfare. Islamists have taken advantage of the shrinking power of these states to develop alternative programs. These shifts have in turn created pressure to open the political system, and cautious steps have been taken in that direction in Jordan, Kuwait, and even (to a much lesser degree) in Saudi Arabia.[44]

In each of these cases, the impetus for political liberalization was a crisis in regime legitimacy, originating in economic failure and felt both within the regime and in the general population. But these countries pose a significant challenge to the post–cold war maxim that economic reform (commonly identified in the West with market reform) and democratization are inextricably linked. In general terms, some studies have found correlations between per capita income (which is usually attributed to economic development) and a society's tendency to democratize. Some have proposed thresholds that correspond to democratic transitions or that help new democracies consolidate.[45] However, these conclusions are based on data from the recent Third Wave of democratic transitions, while the remaining authoritarian holdouts, as noted above, have characteristics that may distinguish them from these new democracies. Moreover, the time lines involved in the economic development of Third Wave countries are so broad it is difficult to point to specific examples of cause and effect. However, it is clear in many remaining authoritarian states that economic reform (or its need) has created pressure for political change, although no clear or uniform path (much less a standard outcome) for such change has been established. Economic reform that fails, or that succeeds but produces obvious and severe inequities, can stir popular protest and force the regime to tolerate greater openness. Conversely, it may cause rulers to clamp down on personal and political freedoms.

Neither can external factors dictate the course of political change, although they are usually taken into account, positively or negatively, in the regime's calculus. Some, although not many, decisions to liberalize have been influenced by changes in the country's international status. De-recognition of Taiwan in the late 1970s, which enabled the United States to recognize the People's Republic of China, helped convince the Kuomintang Party that a more liberal political climate would enhance Taiwan's status in the international community. The loss of Moscow as an economic patron in the late 1980s as a result of the dissolution of the Soviet Union spurred Hanoi into reform (although it did not have a commensurate effect in Cuba).

In the post–cold war era, international action is increasingly directed toward the internal affairs of nations. Pressure is building against authoritarian regimes of all stripes, through conditionality (or its threat) on aid and trade; the growing trend toward multilateral intervention to halt internal conflict, particularly that which results from authoritarian abuse; and increased international involvement in bringing large-scale human rights abusers to justice. Global media intensify this pressure, giving citizens greater awareness of world events and enhanced means to interact with the outside world, as well as with one another. Although these global trends are likely only to increase in influence, they have not yet produced the large-scale impact of the de-recognition of Taiwan or Vietnam's loss of a major economic sponsor, and the impact is still modest.

A related factor is the demonstration effect. The decision to initiate or allow a liberalization process is an intensely internal one, but it would be misguided to assume that the fates of other authoritarian regimes have no impact. Authoritarian leaders in Asia sought to contain media coverage in their countries of Suharto's fall in Indonesia, but it is doubtful they missed the lesson of that fall—that excessively brittle regimes are likely to break.[46] Chinese leadership was clearly affected by the collapse of the Soviet bloc, although its conclusions about the ramifications of the collapse are the opposite of those of Western ideologues. Western democrats tend to stress the initial victory for democracy in the liberation of Eastern Europe and the demise of the Soviet Union. Chinese elites, as well as many ordinary citizens, point instead to the political, economic, and ethnic chaos that followed. The regimes considered in this study tend to see themselves as more entrenched than those of personal rulers such as Suharto and more resilient than the rigid leadership that characterized the Soviet model. For these leaders, the near-term aim of liberalization is to reshape the system—to improve policy-making and accommodate new interest groups—without replacing it.

The Need for a New Policy

It is in the United States' interest to encourage these experiments in liberalization, however limited, to move in a positive direction and to help consolidate their gains. Whether or not it leads to democratization, liberalization carries with it the possibility of greater openness and improved human rights. In some cases it may move society closer to a rule of law, although that is rarely secured during the liberalization period. Any improvements in these areas ultimately stand to benefit the international community as well as the individual society. Conversely, a liberalization effort that meets a bad end or a serious obstacle can have a profound impact on the country's foreign as well as domestic affairs. A classic example was the downward spiral in China's relations with the West after the suppression of the Tiananmen Square movement in 1989. Another, more far-reaching, example was the shah of Iran's ill-fated attempts at liberalization in the late 1970s, largely at U.S. urging, and the subsequent Islamic Revolution.[47] Because it is controlled initially by a small group of individuals, liberalization can be a closed and arbitrary process in the early stages. Nevertheless, a measured policy to support it can, if it does not threaten the regime and capsize the effort, help keep the process on course, allowing time for the gains of liberalization to accumulate.

But a policy to reinforce and expand these new openings must begin with an awareness—of current trends and conditions in these countries and of the nature of liberalization—that is largely lacking in the present U.S. policy framework. A new policy requires recognition of liberalization as a process separate from that of democratization, for however short or long a time, and actors and instruments different from those used in democracy promotion.

In this policy paradigm, liberalization must be detached from the democratic imperative, which assumes political freedoms that are anathema to many of these regimes.

Although it should not be seen as an endorsement of authoritarian rule, a policy to reinforce liberalizing trends must take into account the reasons why authoritarianism has endured in these countries and why it is now under pressure to reform. In that regard, renewed efforts in both scholarship and policy analysis are needed to support this paradigm shift. Inquiry into the conditions that now foster (or discourage) authoritarianism must be revived and updated to repair a long break.

Not surprisingly, typology is usually determined by the prevailing views of the times. Working parallel to policymakers, the academic community has focused primarily on the process of democratization in the 1990s. In the 1960s, the large-scale reversal of the many post-colonial democratic experiments, coupled with pitched competition between the world's two major political blocs, gave rise to a body of work in the 1970s that attempted to classify authoritarian regimes.[48] The right-wing regimes studied (most of which were in Latin America) were those that had fallen back from some stage of democratization.[49] Attempting to counter this political aphasia, or return to repression, "redemocratization" was articulated as a U.S. policy goal.

Because Leninist regimes were largely out of reach, scholarship on them did not give rise to useful policy prescriptions to promote internal change. (It is difficult to imagine, however, what U.S. policy measures could possibly have affected the course of Chinese political development during the Cultural Revolution of the 1960s and early 1970s, when relations were severed and the United States and China were in military conflict by proxy through the Vietnam War.) And while there was greater attention to communist regimes during the cold war than at the present time, there was also an assumption that they uniformly followed the Soviet model in architecture if not always in political loyalty.[50]

These directions in scholarly research reemerged in policy during the early 1980s with the Kirkpatrick Doctrine, which provided the intellectual underpinnings for the Reagan administration's policies toward left- and right-wing totalitarian and authoritarian regimes. The doctrine maintained that repressive regimes on the left (that is, communist ones) were incapable of evolving into more benign forms and that right-wing regimes offered greater hope for political reform. This distinction helped to freeze in place a relative lack of attention to prospects for liberalization among Leninist regimes.[51] Vestiges of this view can be found in both official policy and American public opinion twenty years later. For example, a recent survey indicated that Americans consider China to be significantly more repressive than Saudi Arabia,[52] which runs counter to global surveys of human rights protection for the past several years.

For a brief period, events in the latter half of the 1980s encouraged more mottled views of political change and regime type. Gorbachev's dual program of economic and political reforms, which also signaled that reform regimes would be permitted in the Eastern European satellites, was beginning to unravel the Kirkpatrick Doctrine. Many Latin American and some Asian countries on the other end of the political spectrum also underwent periods of liberalization, which eventually produced democratic transitions. In China, Deng Xiaoping's reforms (which predated Gorbachev's in conception, if not always in execution) were beginning to take hold. In response to this widespread loosening of political systems, social scientists attempted to differentiate between varieties of totalitarian regimes and to flesh out the definition of authoritarianism. One leading study, for example, identified nine types of authoritarian regimes: traditional, military, bureaucratic, corporatist, racial or ethnic "democracy," post-totalitarian, mobilizational, personalistic, and populist.[53] Of course, many hybrid regimes exist as well, such as bureaucratic-military (Thailand before 1998) and personalistic-military (Nigeria for most of its post-independence history). But just as study of authoritarianism in the late 1970s focused on the disintegration of democracy, scholars in the late 1980s tended to be more interested in liberalizing regimes that were clearly headed for democratic transitions.[54]

Because a number of states have indeed moved toward democracy since the beginning of the 1990s, the attempt to calibrate political systems on the authoritarian end of the spectrum has been largely abandoned. No new studies have been launched with the scope equivalent to those of the 1980s. Inquiry into nondemocratic states was scaled back because of the need to give greater attention to democratizing regimes, which appeared to pop up daily in the years immediately after the cold war. The only comprehensive regime project that carried over from that decade reverted in the 1990s to a monolithic definition of authoritarian government and chose to forgo a distinction even between totalitarian and authoritarian rule. For example, in a database extending through 1992, China is shown as having undergone no regime change at all during the course of its modern political history, on par with North Korea.[55]

The literature on individual countries cannot help but take a more detailed approach to political change. As a result, what current study there is of liberalization tends to be embedded in these works. Among the countries of greatest concern to this study, the most extensive body of literature is on China, building upon twenty years of reform, episodic though that reform may be.[56] Because reform efforts in Vietnam and Iran are more recent and foreign analysts have less access to indigenous officials and local scholars, the literature on political conditions in these countries is sparse by comparison. But the relative wealth of information on China is not sufficient in itself to enable policymakers to identify and understand the phenomenon of political liberalization as it is presently taking place in these countries. More comparative study is needed, as well as more stringent analysis of the efforts of external actors to influence these regimes.

It is beyond the scope of this book to contribute to the theoretical understanding of the process of liberalization through a large-scale comparative project, nor can it provide detailed data on each of the liberalizing regimes presently of concern to the United States. Instead, this study pursues three essential tasks. Chapters 2 and 3 delineate the process of political liberalization in some of the present "hold-out" countries, from the perspective of both the regime and civil society. China serves as a prominent example in these studies, with illustrations from other countries where possible. Chapter 4 evaluates present U.S. policy to promote political change in these countries and argues that it is seriously out of synch with the liberalization process. Chapter 5 concludes with the proposal for a policy to encourage positive change in these countries that is a pragmatic approach to the pursuit of moral goals.

2

The "Right" Thing for the "Wrong" Reason: When Rulers Reform

Alexis de Tocqueville, who has enjoyed a revival among scholars in the post–cold war period, observed that "the most perilous moment for a bad government is one when it seeks to mend its ways."[1] Authoritarian rulers who initiate or accede to political reforms are well aware of this principle. As a result, they are most likely to agree to liberalization when it serves the purposes of the regime as well as those of other interests. This purpose may be broad, such as renewing legitimacy for the ruling elite with the general population, or narrow, such as appeasing and co-opting reformist elements within the regime. The dual nature of liberalization, which cynics might describe as rulers doing the "right" thing for the "wrong" reason, ensures that it will be an uncertain, uneven process.

The fundamental uncertainty of liberalization lies in the mid to long term. Whatever motives drive their decisions, regimes are reluctant to allow openings unless they are confident that they will be able to control them. They may even choose to initiate reforms, hoping that a paternalistic approach to political change will be a more secure one for the ruling order.[2] Under these conditions, the short-term outcome—measured in less than a decade—is usually continued dominance by the incumbents, although state, society, and the ruling group itself may be tacitly transformed. During this period the pace of liberalization can be easily checked, as seen in the recent slowdowns of the late 1990s in Vietnam and Laos, intended to head off social unrest caused by spillover from the Asian economic crisis.[3] History has shown, however, that the end result of liberalization may take many forms, often unforeseen by the reformers themselves.

Rulers may miscalculate their own strength or popular appeal and permit the process to slip beyond the point of easy control. This can ultimately lead to the departure of the regime, whether or not it is replaced by more democratic leadership. In other cases it can prompt a return to more repressive rule as the regime regains its hold. For Ferdinand Marcos, the decision to allow elections in the Philippines in 1986 was a fatal error, not only because he failed to maintain a popular mandate at the polls, but (more important) because he had underestimated the organization of civil watchdog groups, a force that prevented him from nullifying the election by fraud. In 1990 the military-backed State Law and Order Reconciliation Council (SLORC) in Burma permitted free elections to go forward because it had seriously miscalculated the military's popularity. When it lost in a landslide, SLORC set aside the election results and called a halt to further political reform.

Not every abortive attempt at liberalization is seen in the black-and-white terms in which the international community viewed the Burmese election—as a dialectic of freedom versus repression. The complications of political change are illustrated by the four-year period of political relaxation in Algeria during the late 1980s and early 1990s. This liberal opening saw the sudden upsurge of an Islamist opposition, the Islamic Salvation Front (FIS), which seemed likely to prevail in elections. Convinced that the FIS would install a repressive government and call a halt to further reforms, the military intervened to stop the electoral process. The Algerian dilemma has been debated extensively by policymakers and scholars, many of whom see in it a cautionary tale for other Muslim-majority countries. Those who supported the regime's actions maintain that the military helped to preserve Algeria's prospects for democracy by preventing the installation of a group that they believe would have returned the country to authoritarian rule under different guise. Their opponents insist that the cancellation of elections served only to further radicalize Islamist parties and perpetuate internal violence. Both sides, however, acknowledge that too rapid a process of liberalization can be destabilizing, by placing disparate forces into competition for political power when there is little agreement on the new rules of the game.[4] There is precedent for this seeming turn against democracy in the cold war. In the 1950s, for example, the United States opposed holding a transitional free election for the whole of Vietnam, as required under the 1954 Geneva Accords, because it believed that the North Vietnamese Communist Party, the Viet Minh, would be able to engineer an electoral victory through intimidation.

Since 1992 Algeria has seen the resumption of liberalization but in a more cautious and exclusionary form. Presidential elections were conducted in 1995 and parliamentary elections in 1997, the latter producing the first multiparty parliament in Algerian history. Several moderate Islamist parties were allowed to contest, but participation by the FIS was prohibited.[5] By compartmentalizing liberalization in this way, the government is hoping to extinguish the appeal of the FIS through political starvation.[6]

This policy is consonant with new trends in the Middle East toward the inclusion of moderate Islamist groups in the political process and even toward increased dialogue with more radical factions.[7] Some analysts maintain that, under this new policy of cautious openness, Islamist movements can be a force for democratic expansion. In Jordan, for example, the liberalization trend that began in 1989 caused Islamist groups to embrace democracy as a political strategy.[8] Although Islamists in Jordan have thus far demonstrated more moderate inclinations than their Algerian counterparts did in 1992, there are still serious risks attendant on this approach. Liberalization in Jordan has opened the political system to a wide range of opposition parties, not only the Islamist groups, and the resultant competition has broken the Islamist monopoly on opposition power. This could eventually force Islamist groups into more radical positions, as could the growing Palestinian character of the Islamist movement in Jordan.[9]

In some cases a liberalization experiment may be terminated because it has fulfilled the regime's immediate aims and helped to restore the ruling elite's power under new circumstances. A classic example of this use of liberalization was Mao Tse-tung's Hundred Flowers Campaign in the 1950s, in which the population was encouraged to voice criticisms of the party. In this way, the party was able to root out and punish the ideologically incorrect. In the Anti-Rightist Campaign that followed, more than 800,000 Chinese were sentenced to "reform through labor" for political crimes.[10]

Most examples of this bait-and-switch approach are less catastrophic. In 1989 Suharto initiated a five-year period of relative openness (*keterbukaan*) in Indonesia. During this time he relaxed censorship of the press, allowed some public demonstrations, and created a small number of institutions— such as the National Commission for Human Rights—that had the potential to check executive power through public criticism. In doing so, he was able to pursue a sub rosa strategy of reshuffling the military to his advantage, by using openness to deepen factions within the armed forces, increasing support for the regime with Muslim organizations, and gauging the prospects for his continued, open-ended presidency. By 1994 these objectives had essentially been met, removing the need to tolerate anti-regime criticism. When the press leveled corruption charges against officials close to Suharto, he cut short *keterbukaan*.[11]

It is impossible to determine how long the Suharto regime would have survived had the Asian financial crisis not thrust the Indonesian economy into a downturn in 1997. However, the events which turned Suharto out of power in 1998 suggest that some of the gains of the *keterbukaan* period survived the 1994 crackdown. For example, the National Commission for Human Rights, which had grown steadily in strength and reputation through the 1990s, played a central role in criticizing the regime's handling of student demonstrations, undermining the perception of Suharto as a legitimate ruler. More important, the Muslim organizations that had been able to build grassroots support during *keterbukaan* emerged as leading actors in the political drama of 1998, which culminated in Suharto's downfall.[12]

Liberal openings that do not end precipitously in the short-term usually follow one of two paths. Some produce stable, semi-authoritarian systems in which the prospects for further political reform are stalled indefinitely. Uganda and Ethiopia are often cited as examples of this phenomenon in Africa, as well as Egypt and Tunisia in the Middle East. Semi-authoritarian states in Asia such as Singapore and Malaysia have representative and judicial systems that, although democratic on paper, are frequently used to protect and preserve the regime through authoritarian practices.[13] Russia is likely to remain in a state of limbo between authoritarianism and democracy for several years to come.

Some liberalization efforts have led directly and peacefully to democratic transitions, although it has often taken a generation to reach that point. The most successful have been those in which the regime was able to manage the pace of change while meeting the expectations of a widening spectrum of social and political interests and in which the regime itself became convinced that democratization was an appropriate step. The transition out of authoritarianism in Franco's Spain and the move away from military rule in Brazil are examples of this kind of incremental political development.[14]

Transitions that are more contentious and tumultuous often have an element of managed change as well. In the late 1980s President Roh Tae Woo, himself a former military officer, signaled that a sea change in Korean politics was required when he publicly urged that his successor be a civilian.[15]

Even when the path from authoritarianism to democracy is relatively unbroken, these transitions often involve a change of regime early in the democratization process. In the case of Taiwan, however, the move from totalitarian to authoritarian rule, and later to democracy, was managed by the Kuomintang Party (KMT), which retained power well past the transitional elections. This pattern requires a profound transformation not only of state and society but also of the regime itself. Although relatively rare, it may have relevance and appeal to some of the focus countries in this study, particularly the Asian Leninist states, since it appears to offer some degree of continuity and stability.[16]

Experiments in liberalization may differ in their objectives and outcome, but they all tend to be uneven in their execution. A surge too far forward—by regime reformers, civil society organizations, or opposition groups—is likely to be pulled back by ruling hard-liners, or by moderates seeking to prevent reforms from being canceled altogether. Conversely, a significant move toward openness may be prefaced by a period of increased control, to assure the regime (and remind reformers) of its continued power. For example, the democratic opening in Taiwan in 1986 was preceded by two years of tightened press censorship.[17] This spasmodic movement, more elegantly known as the "reform tango," can confuse and frustrate outside observers and make it difficult to discern the ultimate direction of political change.

Regimes are also uneven in their distribution of the benefits of liberalization. Promoting openness across the board is the task of the democratization process. The most that liberalization will tolerate is the presence of enclaves of openness, in the formal system or in civil society. For example, local elections in Taiwan were permitted for decades before national leadership could be elected,[18] a sequence that some analysts believe will eventually play out in China. Authorized in the 1950s well before the liberalization era of the late 1970s and early 1980s, their purpose was twofold: to start Taiwan down a long road toward "guided democracy," as KMT founder Sun Yat-sen had envisioned, and to bind the Taiwanese to a party whose leadership was composed primarily of mainlanders and who maintained tight control of the national legislature. A more basic process is unfolding in the

Gulf state of Qatar, where representative government has been initiated at the local level through the establishment of a municipal council structure considered to be the forerunner of a national parliament. It is perhaps auspicious that women are allowed to vote and to run for the municipal council, in contrast to both Kuwait and Saudi Arabia.[19]

A reverse sequence has been in play in Iran. National elections preceded local ones, because the process for nomination of national candidates ensured that all potential winners would be drawn from the ruling hierarchy. (The 1997 presidential election, however, revealed a wider spectrum within that hierarchy than had been assumed.) Although they were envisioned in the political plan put forward by the regime after the 1979 revolution, local elections were not implemented in Iran until 1999.[20] However, as the reform movement in Iran has consolidated, distinctions between national and local elections have diminished. The 2000 parliamentary elections returned a resoundingly reformist majority (75 percent), in contrast to the 1996 parliamentary polls and very much in keeping with the 1997 elections and 1999 local contests.

Generally, liberalizing regimes tend to grant rights and favors to those groups that are least likely to encourage an organized opposition. They disadvantage or discourage potential rivals for political power, although power-sharing often occurs to some degree in other realms, such as economic policy, where an infusion of apolitical technocrats is common. Certain civil society groups that can mobilize critical elements of the population, such as labor unions, are also subject to the tighter controls.

These mechanisms for regime control make the gains of liberalization ambiguous and fragile. In contrast to the democratization process, in which representative institutions become stronger and civil society more autonomous, reformers in authoritarian systems must operate in political and social spaces that are minimal and tightly controlled. Nevertheless, even on this smaller scale significant gains are still possible.

Moderates and Middlemen

Many Westerners who hope to encourage trends toward openness in authoritarian systems assume that the agents of political change are to be found in outspoken intellectuals or other activists and beleaguered, would-be opposition parties. Progress is therefore measured by the extent to which these actors are permitted to operate and their impact on the political system.[21] This view also assumes the authoritarian regime to be a monolith–increasingly brittle and anachronistic. There is little evidence, however, to support this model of political change in several of the liberalizing states of Asia and the Middle East. On the contrary, current trends suggest that the greatest (and, in the early stages, the only) political pluralism in the liberalization process is intramural, occurring within the regime itself.

Scholars have long noted that the decision to reform is frequently a matter of debate, struggle, and alliance-building between regime conservatives, or hard-liners, and regime progressives, who by objective measures might best be termed moderates.[22] In the early stages of liberal reform, the very appearance of moderates who diverge from the traditional hard line might be considered progress, however they fare. Once they do emerge, factionalism often proliferates. By the late Deng Xiaoping era in China, for example, the spectrum in the party leadership was relatively wide and included constitutional reformers who, although not seeking to overturn one-party rule, advocated legal reform, greater social pluralism, and more rational decision-making; mainstreamers who discouraged open political debate but tolerated more divergent views in other areas of policy; new authoritarians, who resembled mainstreamers but were less permissive on debate over economic policy; Marxist fundamentalists, who remained loyal to Soviet-style communism; and ultranationalists, who attempted to fill the ideological gap at the end of the cold war with nationalism as a justification for party rule.[23] In the other Asian Leninist states, the ruling order is broadening but is not nearly as ventilated as the Chinese political elite. For example, decision-making within the Vietnamese Communist Party has historically been more collective, and the need for consensus can sand down points of disagreement before they can be more fully developed.[24]

An equally complex spectrum is evident in the present-day political elite of Iran. In the wake of the economic failure of the 1980s, the regime first exhibited a split between fundamentalists and conservatives. The former are the political old guard, who adhere to the 1979 vision of an Islamic society guided by trained experts in religious law and ethics and who retain a number of influential positions in the ruling structure. By contrast, conservatives are more concerned with politics and specific areas of policymaking rather than the theological underpinnings of government. Since they include the *bazaari* (big business) class in their political constituency, they tend to focus on economic issues.[25] Although comparisons are generally ill advised, this post-1979 split might be likened to the divisions that emerged in the early Deng Xiaoping era in China. With the more open political system of the late 1990s, a more progressive substratum of moderates, reformers, and radicals has emerged in the ruling structure in Iran, forming a loose, pro-reform coalition. The moderate faction, composed of technocrats, advocates government intervention in the economy to help balance growth and to promote free market principles. Reformers are less concerned with economics and more focused on a new Islamic vision of civil society, which has as its base the rule of law. Radicals, on the other hand, double-back to the 1979 revolution and advocate a more pluralistic system as a means of ensuring that the government redistributes wealth as required by Islamic law.[26] Both the Chinese and Iranian spectrums demonstrate not only increased tolerance for differing political positions within a controlled group but also the growing dominance of pragmatists over ideologues.

As reform continues, regime progressives might be expected to proliferate and to gain significant leadership positions, tipping the balance of power toward the advocates of change. During this time, individual leaders may also modify their political positions and move closer toward the liberal end of the spectrum. And as liberalization continues, each successive leader is expected to outdo his predecessor's reforms and so strives to emphasize his reformist credentials. When these changes become visible to outside observers, the international community often assumes that a political watershed has been reached, as many believe to have been the case in Iran with the election of Khatami as president.

But the crucial process of regime infighting and coalition-building can be difficult for observers to follow and understand, all the more so in an era that assumes global democratization. Once liberalization is launched in an authoritarian system and the regime displays obvious fissures, Western observers are often tempted to underestimate the strength of hard-liners and to oversell the influence of moderates. They may also be premature in declaring hard-line factions to be waning or extinct. In Iran, for example, hard-liners continue to control the judiciary.[27] In China, the emphatic reemergence of dominant conservatives following the Tiananmen Square crackdown surprised many Americans. Moreover, hard-line elements can regenerate, as seen by the surge of young conservatives into leadership positions in China in the early 1990s, dubbed the "party princes and princesses" because they were the children and grandchildren of founding party members.[28]

On the opposite end of the spectrum, Westerners frequently assume that all moderates are democracy activists at heart. Some indeed may have democratic leanings, or aspirations for greater power in a more open political process. However, during the early stages of liberalization they are more likely to be regime faithfuls who believe that reform is necessary to retain legitimacy and power. International democracy promoters are often disillusioned when confronted with this fact.[29] This problem is exacerbated by the opaque and secretive character of most authoritarian regimes. Decisions within the leadership to move toward (or away from) greater openness must often be deduced by outsiders through inference.[30] In times of particular flux, the process may be all but indecipherable from the outside.

The tension between hard-liners and moderates is seldom mitigated during the liberalization period. It frequently continues into the democratization process, where, if fundamental agreement on political reform is not found, it may present a serious threat. In the wake of the Third Wave, numerous democratizing countries in Africa, Asia, and Latin America discovered that yesterday's hard-liners may be tomorrow's coup plotters. However, this tension is a necessary force in liberalization, because it continuously feeds the need to seek policy concessions and keeps the door open for reform. Although these concessions seldom produce single dramatic steps forward, they can generate substantial progress when sustained over a period of time.[31]

As liberalization progresses, the dialogue between conservatives and progressives often radiates outward. Regime members may seek advice on reforms from experts in semi-independent research institutes or other individuals deemed by the regime to be reliable. Commissioned research on potential reforms (or simply the knowledge that it has been requested) may then circulate, creating a low-level public dialogue in which the regime may profess to take no position. The quasi-nongovernmental nature of these research bodies also gives the regime some measure of deniability, avoiding the impression that the reforms under study are actual agenda items.

Exercises such as these are usually discounted by Western activists, who view them as whitewashes because they are conducted by institutions with links to the state. However, they often increase the regime's tolerance for discussion of sensitive issues. In the 1990s, the Chinese government commissioned a series of white papers on human rights, which Western activists initially condemned as an attempt merely to counter international criticism of Beijing's human rights record. Notwithstanding that obvious possibility, the papers' circulation inside China has helped remove the taboo on mention or discussion of human rights. Some international human rights groups now view this process as a net gain for openness, if by a very slim margin.[32] The party has recently been reported to have commissioned comparative studies of political systems, including different forms of democracy.[33] Debate and discussion usually run several years ahead of actual reform, but the mere existence of this discourse, albeit regime-driven, can contribute to a more open political atmosphere.

Regimes may also change during liberalization in their makeup and the nature of their membership. Post–cold war leaders across the political spectrum are increasingly becoming aware that their legitimacy derives less from ideology or tradition than from economic performance, as Suharto's ouster clearly showed. Market economies require leaders and bureaucrats who can make complex economic and administrative decisions, skills not usually held by ideologically driven officials in centrally planned economies or by high-ranking military leaders in right-wing authoritarian regimes.

To meet this need, regimes overseeing economic reforms are often forced to recruit new members with technocratic rather than political credentials. Equally important, for economic reasons they often acquiesce to reforms of the bureaucracy that loosen their monopoly over government personnel. Technocratically minded reformers are becoming more visible in the Iranian political structure. In China in the 1990s, a generation of technocrats began to rise to the upper ranks of government, with mixed results for the party. On the one hand, this new breed of leaders has helped make party rule more efficient, which the leadership hopes will strengthen its legitimacy. On the other, some argue that it has changed the character of the regime, from a party that once claimed to be the vanguard of the proletariat, to a national elite with methods and aims that contradict the fundamental goals of the revolution.[34] A similar dichotomy is developing within China's bureaucracy. The Civil Service Provisional Regulation of 1993 has essentially split the bureaucracy, creating two levels: a cadre of civil servants selected by examination and advanced according to meritocratic, professional criteria, alongside administrators appointed and promoted by the party apparatus.[35]

It would be overreaching to assume that the infusion of technocrats into a ruling structure and bureaucracy will automatically aid political liberalization or that technocrats themselves always support political reform. The evidence in countries undergoing economic reform has been mixed. As with other aspects of liberalization, the deciding factor is the regime's use of this innovation. In Indonesia in the 1960s, Suharto did not employ his "Berkeley mafia" of economists as an instrument for political reform; on the contrary, they helped consolidate his personal rule. But in Thailand in the early 1980s, Prime Minister Prem Tinsulanond, the military-appointed ruler and himself a former armed forces supreme commander, used the appointment of technocrats in his cabinet as a means of moving away from strict military rule. Over the decade, these technocrats proved to be the middlemen between authoritarian and more democratic leaders. In the late 1980s, Prem continued his blend-in approach, salting his cabinet with elected members of Parliament as a way of moving from technocratic to democratic rule. This led to the election of a civilian government in 1988.[36]

In a system undergoing political reform (even one that lags significantly behind economic reform), a technocratic turn can have several positive effects. First, it can further ventilate the regime, creating more internal space in which to bargain for reforms. Second, it can encourage pragmatic decisionmaking, rather than a process that is purely ideological or solely in the regime's self-interest. Third, through bureaucratic reform it can help separate the regime from the state, a relationship that under strict authoritarian rule tends to be closely interwoven. These effects not only diminish the regime's overall control but may also have profound implications for the very system of governance. The first may advance pluralism within the regime, but the last carries with it the seeds of a more profound and far-reaching institutional pluralism.

Reforming Rubber Stamps

In some of the liberalizing states of this study, reform has extended beyond the immediate confines of the political regime. Key institutions are also changing, albeit in an unplanned and episodic fashion. Legislatures are becoming more assertive in China and Vietnam, as well as in some traditional Middle Eastern states. The judicial and legal systems of China are also undergoing subtle transformation. Movement toward a rule of law is not as brisk in the other Leninist states, where neither market reform nor political liberalization are as advanced. Neither is there equal momentum toward legal reform in Middle Eastern states, where the tendency to unite religion and state brings particular complications to judicial and legal reform. On the contrary, as fortresses of conservatism these sectors may block reforms.

In a broader sense, institutional reform in many Middle Eastern states is caught in crosscurrents of social custom and religious law that defy Western prescriptions for political change. Traditional monarchies are particularly resistant to the notion of bottom-up reform. The prototypes for legislatures in many of these countries are privy councils, in which only members of the extended royal family or other representatives of the privileged class venture opinions on public issues. As legal systems have developed, they have tended to take religious law as their base, leaving judicial administration to the clergy rather than secular officials and further marginalizing the law-making powers of the legislature.

Arguably the most tangled and complicated system is found in Iran. The year 2000 elections have been judged free and fair on the whole, but the expectation in the regime is that these contests will preserve a conservative majority. The legal system, although based in Islamic law, retains some elements of pre-1979 practice, such as the right to a public trial and the right to counsel. In addition, like the remaining Leninist states, Iran must also cope with lingering revolutionary frameworks. Judges are still appointed for their ideological beliefs. Acting as both judge and prosecutor, they can serve as political instruments. Indictments are still handed down for "antirevolutionary behavior" or "siding with global arrogance."[37] In a more coordinated effort, after the 2000 parliamentary elections, in which the political character of the legislature moved dramatically toward the reform end of the spectrum, alarmed conservatives used the judiciary to close several pro-reform newspapers.[38]

In the countries of this study, the reform of legislatures is usually a matter of recasting existing institutions. In some states, however, such as the Middle Eastern monarchies of Saudi Arabia and Qatar, liberalization may mean building a legislative framework for the first time. In either case, legislatures and other deliberative bodies are often described politely in constitutions as the highest authority in the land. In reality, they are more likely to be political *cul de sacs*, deriving their legitimacy from the regime so as to affirm its continued monopoly of power. Members are often selected by appointment or by highly limited contests in which both the rules and the results are controlled by the executive branch. Their legislative function is usually restricted to reviewing laws drafted by the regime, which are understood to be approved in advance. Like the executive branches of regimes, moreover, legislatures can take on a corporatist character, particularly when they have protracted or open-ended tenures. The "long parliament" in Laos, for example, lasted more than a decade.

But regardless of their limitations, deliberative bodies in authoritarian states are the primary institutions that link the state to the people. As such, their potential in the liberalization process is twofold. They can invigorate internal competition with shifts away from regime control, however slight, and they can strengthen popular participation through shifting member-constituent relations. Although these trends may not approach the threshold of democratization, it is often during the liberalization period that the principles of checks and balances in government and accountability to the people begin to assume any meaningful form in the political system.

In traditional systems, these bodies may lack even token legislative powers. Their functions may be consultative, enabling them to offer nonbinding opinions on policy decisions; representative, in the sense that members are chosen to reflect the society's mix of regional or social groups; or mediational, disseminating government policies to the people and receiving citizens' complaints about government. Even very restricted assemblies, such as the Consultative Councils in Saudi Arabia and Bahrain, can fulfill several of these functions, each of which can serve as a springboard to enhanced power for the legislature in future periods of political reform.[39] In some Gulf monarchies, regimes aim to co-opt real or potential political opposition and more broadly reduce political alienation not only through formal legislative structures but also through more informal mechanisms for dialogue and contact with the royal family. In Kuwait, networks of gathering places (*diwaniyyas*) are maintained where Kuwaitis can regularly discuss politics, air complaints, petition for redress of grievances, and otherwise try to influence the decisionmaking process.[40]

Western activists and editorial writers are inclined to dismiss as rubber stamps any legislature (or judiciary) that is not sufficiently independent to be an effective counterweight to the executive. Under this definition, assemblies in virtually all authoritarian systems, even liberalizing ones, undoubtedly *are* rubber stamps. However, to apply this criterion in all cases is to ignore, or miss, the evolutionary process that delineates and distances state organs from the regime as a prelude to greater autonomy. This view also simplifies and romanticizes the process of institutional development. Harking back to the struggles of the European middle class against their monarchies, many Westerners view legislative development as a succession of defiant acts in which the assembly brings the executive to heel.[41]

As with other processes of liberalization, legislative development during this period is replete with contradictions. In order to carve out greater autonomy, assemblies must maintain the trust (and accept the bottom-line control) of the regime, not only to avoid reprisal but also to maximize their role in the policymaking process. They must avoid being marginalized if they are to accumulate greater authority and a wider array of state functions. They must also retain adequate support from the regime to operate in a political climate that is often highly personalized. Because the early stages of liberalization tend to be dominated by individual personalities, institutional development may depend upon the regime's willingness to appoint respected, high-ranking figures to the legislature. For these reasons, in the late 1980s reform-minded academics and bureaucrats in China argued that continuation of the close, symbiotic relationship between the state and party was a short-term necessity. They calculated that attempts to gain immediate independence for the legislature or judiciary would result in the isolation of those institutions and their exclusion from power-sharing.[42]

Despite these conditions, and because of them, national and provincial legislatures in both China and Vietnam have been able to expand their capacity and reach in the 1990s. This has been accomplished through a combination of constitutional reform (in 1982 in China and in 1992 in Vietnam) that granted increased powers to the legislatures to support market reform and opportunistic leaps on the part of the legislators themselves.

Over the past twenty years, legislative output in the Chinese National People's Congress (NPC), measured by laws and resolutions passed or amended, has doubled. Beyond this broad measure of capacity, recent data also suggest that the NPC is gradually becoming more assertive as well. Contradicting traditions of absolute party management of the legislature, NPC deputies are proposing new legislation, debating and amending laws introduced by the party, and, on rare occasions, openly voting against some of the government's highest legislative priorities in significant (if not winning) proportions.[43]

For example, in 1992 a small but vocal contingent in the NPC voted against or abstained on the government's proposal for the Three Gorges Dam project. When opponents of the bill were silenced by the Chairman's Committee during debate, they resorted to handing out pamphlets in the corridors.[44] In 1995 more than a third of the deputies voted against the People's Bank Law, and a quarter against the Education Law. Deputies have also become more outspoken in refusing to approve annual government reports upon occasion and opposing some party nominations for high posts, two areas in which the NPC's role had historically been pro forma. A parallel trend is emerging at the provincial level, with reports of Provincial Congresses that have rejected some party nominations for governors and elected write-in candidates.[45] These minor watersheds are more complex than they appear because they suggest a change in the party as well as the legislature. Not only are deputies taking discernible, if modest, steps toward increased autonomy, but they are doing so with the expectation that they will not suffer reprisal from the regime. This assumption was given an institutional boost in 1998 with the establishment of an anonymous voting system in the NPC.[46] At this juncture, anonymity serves the cause of liberalization because it helps shield legislators from party surveillance. By contrast, in the democratization process, reformers often lobby to remove this protection and make votes public in order to hold the legislature more accountable to the people.

The indications of a more assertive legislature in a liberalizing system are usually attitudinal shifts and other signs that are difficult to quantify. Like the party itself, the composition of the Chinese NPC is beginning to tilt toward reformers. From 1978 to 1993, the representation of intellectuals and technocrats in the legislature rose from 28 to 50 percent. During the same period, the strength of more traditional deputies—workers, peasants, and officers of the People's Liberation Army—fell from a combined total of 62 percent to roughly half that size.[47] Moreover, observers note visible changes in the NPC's daily business and a determination to turn the customary tangle of rules, regulations, and party dicta into a coherent body of law.[48] To support this new sense of mission, deputies have called for increased access to information and for more trained professional staff.[49]

Equally important, albeit less tangible, is the shift in self-image on the part of a growing number of deputies. Legislators who would have viewed themselves as agents of the state ten years ago now see themselves as representatives of constituents, on broad matters of policy as well as specific interests. A corresponding shift is seen in the population of ordinary Chinese, measured by a rising tide of letters and petitions to the NPC, as private citizens turn to their national and provincial assemblies for assistance on a wide range of matters that would previously have been directed to party officials or bureaucrats.[50]

In comparison to China, the Vietnamese political ethic of strong party unity, if only on the surface, has built greater restraint into the reform process. In its official rhetoric, the Vietnamese Communist Party (VCP) continues to deplore notions of "pluralism" or "peaceful evolution."[51] However, Hanoi, like Beijing, has found the gradual opening of state institutions to be inevitable as it has come to realize that to command is not necessarily to govern. But in contrast to Deng Xiaoping's more comprehensive road map for reform, the politburo in Hanoi did not originally foresee a need for political reform. By the 1990s it was clear to the leadership that policy must be delegated more broadly across the system, in order to maintain support for reform and to address the costs of reform, such as dwindling social services and increased corruption.

The expansion of the Vietnamese National Assembly in the political life of the nation is the most salient sign of this cautious shift. Debate in the legislature on economic, legal, and social issues is increasingly vigorous. In 1997 legislators not only questioned and criticized ministers but managed to vote down the government's nomination of the ministerial-level chairman of the central bank to serve a new term.[52] The National Assembly's development has had a tangible effect upon the party as well. The VCP has had to develop an "interagency" system to respond to the Assembly's growing inquiries on party policies and decisions.[53] Moreover, the changing relationship between the party and the Assembly has given the public a new point of entry into political affairs. Live television coverage of Assembly debate in recent years, as well as the responses of government officials to the interpellation of Assembly deputies, has spurred public comment on government leaders. Even some state-run newspapers have published the critical responses of television viewers, some of whom characterized officials as uninformed and evasive.[54]

In one of the many paradoxes of liberalization, loosening state institutions from their regime moorings may rebound against reformers. In 1998 the National Assembly refused to approve government-sponsored amendments that would have further reformed Vietnamese land law. One explanation is that the Assembly supported the positions of local leaders (who would have lost significant control over the rural areas under the proposed reforms) because local party officials vet candidates for the NPC.[55] But at bottom the Assembly's boldest institutional move to date served to hand party hard-liners a legislative victory over moderates.

A parallel and perhaps more complicated example occurred in Kuwait in 1999, when the National Assembly rejected the emir's ruling that women should be given full political rights.[56] The substance of the vote notwithstanding, the Assembly's action is one indication of a more assertive legislature, particularly in a conservative monarchy. The Kuwaiti Parliament has changed dramatically in composition as well. It is now dominated by the Islamist and liberal opposition, two groups that the monarchy had previously held at bay. Some members of Parliament chart complex motives in the vote, which illustrates the complications of political reform. They maintain that the emir's ruling was overturned not only because of opposition from Islamist factions in the legislature but also because reformers objected to the government's attempt to rule by decree.[57]

The development of these legislatures in authoritarian systems underscores the difficulty of applying democratic criteria to the process of political liberalization or even of envisioning a common sequence for change from one country to the next. In theoretical terms, China might be considered more "democratic" than Vietnam at this time because NPC deputies may introduce legislation, while their counterparts in Hanoi can only vote on party-drafted laws. On the other hand, Vietnam might be placed ahead of China on the democratic spectrum because its Assembly members are chosen through popular election, albeit with a nomination process controlled by the party, while NPC deputies are selected by lower-level congresses in secret, party-managed balloting. These difficulties suggest that the growth of institutional pluralism in nations moving away from strict authoritarian rule cannot be plotted in linear form. They also indicate that, in both meaning and use, these institutions differ significantly from their counterparts in democratic systems, even as they become more open.

Approaching Rule of Law

A more complicated move toward institutional pluralism, and one that has an immediate impact on the populations of these countries, is found in the attempts of some liberalizing states to promulgate new bodies of law and reform their legal systems. In liberalizing systems, judiciaries often remain subservient to the regime long after legislatures have become more independent. Authoritarian rulers have traditionally employed legal systems to improve the efficiency of a repressive system or to codify the power of a new regime. In imperial China, legal reform was a ritual performed by each new dynasty to soften or erase the imprint of the preceding one. Authoritarian leaders in the twentieth century took up this practice with vigor. In this century, for example, Thailand has had nearly twenty constitutions, roughly corresponding to the number of regime changes, most of them from one military dictatorship to the next.[58]

But in sustained liberalization efforts where changes within the regime and popular pressure combine to demand a more equitable legal process, a society may begin the complex transition to a rule of law. In Western terms, this concept is taken to mean the supremacy of law over the actions of governments as well as citizens and equality of all citizens under the law. Although rule of law is assumed to be integral to the modern state, scholars point out that the West is particularly disposed to it through the Judeo-Christian view of a supreme being as judge and the role of the judge in society as a leader and a hero.[59] Therefore, the functions of law enforcement and adjudication are more naturally separated from the political process.

The cultures in which authoritarian systems now hold sway have seldom exhibited that degree of separation. Islamic government resists a distinction between the religious and the political and assumes that *shari'a* will be the basic law. This foundation makes brisk movement toward rule of law in the Western sense particularly difficult, because there is no clear consensus on the source of new laws or on which institutions have final authority in formulating and interpreting them.[60] In revolutionary Marxist-Leninist systems, legal and judicial functions were centered in vanguard political organizations and used to police citizens for their ideological correctness. As these systems became more corporatist, judicial functions were transferred to the courts, which nevertheless remained an arm and instrument of the party.

Despite these cultural and historical differences, Westerners who urge the rule of law upon authoritarian states often see the reform process as a technical one: building a certain legal infrastructure and rewriting laws to give them specific content.[61] However, a genuine move toward the rule of law must go beyond building new institutions dedicated to legal and judicial functions and must also reform those political structures that have enabled regimes to rule through extralegal and extrajudicial means. It must also reshape the very concept of a legal system, from a one-way street in which the regime's will is systematically imposed upon the people, to a more reciprocal relationship in which citizens are able to defend themselves against the state's arbitrary use of power or the misdeeds of fellow citizens.

In several countries emerging from authoritarianism, usually those undergoing market reform, the initial motivation for legal reform is more pragmatic than ideological. The creation of a market system requires a more disciplined and predictable legal environment to attract domestic and foreign investors. The ability of investors to choose the target and timing of their investments mitigates the unilateral nature of authoritarian rule. Laws that recognize and strengthen property rights, the uniform application of these laws, and mechanisms that enforce contracts and settle disputes in a timely manner are widely regarded as the basic legal infrastructure of a working market system. Foreign investors and their governments are unyielding in demanding that emerging markets meet these standards, as seen in the pressure placed upon China by the United States during the 1980s and 1990s to strengthen intellectual property protection.[62] As a result, early legal reform is often focused on establishing or revising commercial codes and other aspects of law (contract, partnership, real estate, tax, and currency regulation) that bear upon foreign commercial relations. Although pressure of this sort may appear to be unique to the market-intensive environment of the post–cold war era, with security concerns no longer an overriding factor in foreign policy and a large number of new markets available to foreign investors, foreign commercial interests have historically helped to shape legal systems. In Asia during the nineteenth century, even states that avoided outright colonization—Japan, China, and Thailand—were compelled to establish modern legal codes to defend against unequal treaty arrangements with the European powers.

Legal reform intended simply to appease or accommodate foreign investors can be cordoned off from the domestic population for a period of time. However, as market reform continues, regimes are increasingly inclined to include other areas of law in the reform process. This, too, often occurs for practical reasons: to address the consequences of economic change. The shift to a market economy often results in a shrinking state, leaving the regime less capable of directing every area of public life and mediating every dispute. A more systematic legal approach lightens the regime's burden in this regard. In keeping with the two-track nature of liberalization, a more uniform system can help preserve the regime's power in the short term by allowing it to concentrate on political rule. Legal reform may also address the negative consequences of market reform, particularly those that result from rapid economic growth. Because of this, evidence of legal reform is seen more clearly in the liberalizing Asian Leninist states than in the Middle East, where market reform is not as brisk. However, marketization has also been shown in several countries to exacerbate official corruption, risking social unrest, and to increase other areas of crime. In countries attempting simultaneous political and economic transitions, such as Russia, the negative effects of market reform often outpace legal reform in the short run.[63]

A common step after reform of commercial law in many liberalizing states is to amend administrative law in order to hold public officials more accountable and to revise criminal procedures. Change in this area has obvious implications for human rights. Whether criminal law reform is a net gain for freedom often depends upon the degree of openness being fostered across the system as a whole. Authoritarian leaders rarely begin reform movements by strengthening individual rights. However, in a relaxing political environment, consciousness of the property rights of the individual may spill over to awareness of individual rights in the personal and civil realms, and the government may be pressured to strengthen those rights in legal reform.

How far can authoritarian states be expected to move toward the rule of law during the liberalization process? In the post–cold war period, even democratizing states have had obvious difficulty institutionalizing this principle, as seen by the proliferation of "illiberal democracies." In authoritarian systems, legal reform is no less ragged than other aspects of liberalization. Typically, those areas of law that directly challenge the political role of the regime are the last to liberalize, in enforcement if not in form. Thus internal security law, which enables the regime to silence or incarcerate its political enemies, is often maintained or recycled into new law that gives continued latitude to the ruling group.[64]

Legal reform also provides an opportunity for the regime to apply new laws to trends outside the formal sector (such as the emergence of nongovernmental organizations) that were previously unregulated because they had not coalesced to any meaningful degree. This may provide the regime with increased control, but it may also help to legitimate new actors in the system and to establish limits (often generous) on government control over them. In a liberalizing environment, stringent laws may be promulgated, but the test is in their implementation. This was illustrated by China's promulgation of new laws on nongovernmental organizations (NGOs) in 1998. Human rights groups argue that the new regulations curb de facto freedoms that had been carved out by civil society organizations by increasing the number of bureaucratic obstacles to registration and tightening the controls of requisite government "sponsors."[65] On the other hand, some reformers believe that the law is ultimately aimed at preventing the formation of new political parties and will have little impact on nonpolitical groups.[66]

As with other areas of reform, the measure of progress during liberalization is more a matter of direction than destination. Optimally, two important trends may emerge. First, legal reform during a period of openness may narrow the gap between discretionary power and due process through more even enforcement of laws. Second, a two-way flow of legal protection often emerges, which not only offers increased protection to citizens but also enables them to initiate legal actions against government as well as against other citizens. The latter is a complex phenomenon, requiring administrative and legal reform as well as the development of legal aid organizations and other civil society supports. In a best-case scenario, citizens' access to law is expanded, even if their rights under law are not fully secure.

These two trend lines intersect at present in Chinese legal reform, in both the volume and nature of lawsuits before the courts. Despite widespread perceptions of judicial corruption and inefficiency, litigation has skyrocketed in China over the past fifteen years. Through civil and administrative suits, increasing numbers of everyday Chinese are challenging traditional relations between the state and citizens and between employers and workers. Three aspects of legal reform contribute to this phenomenon. First, the development of a body of administrative litigation law, which defines and limits government authority, has enabled citizens to sue the state for infringements and transgressions of those limits. In recent years the largest percentage increase of lawsuits filed have been those brought by citizens against the state or an administrative entity, rising by 48 percent from 1996 to 1997. Of greater significance, two-thirds of the judgments in those cases were decided in favor of the citizen-plaintiff.[67] A further breakdown sheds light on the interplay of economic and political reform at this time. On a proportional basis, private entrepreneurs file more suits against the government than any other social group.[68] The anecdotal evidence of this growing field of law is significant as well. Citizen-litigants have brought cases related to sensitive issues of individual rights, such as illegal detention by police and abuse of family planning law by employers in state-owned enterprises.[69]

A second development is the growth of class action suits in Chinese litigation. Approved for the first time in 1991 under the Civil Procedure Law, class action litigation offers a double benefit in the liberalization process. It can help expand citizens' rights under law through wide-impact cases, and it constitutes a form (admittedly ad hoc) of civil society organization. However, as in other areas, the parameters are largely influenced by the state. The great majority of class action suits taken on by the courts in China have been consistent with central government priorities. For example, growing unemployment and resulting social unrest have prompted Beijing to encourage class action litigation by aggrieved workers as an alternative to public protest or citizen-organized labor unions.[70]

Finally, rule of law in China has been strengthened by the increasing privatization and professionalization of the legal sector. Reforms in the mid-1990s permitted the establishment of private law partnerships, and private firms now make up approximately one-third of all law firms in China. Some observers speculate that this trend will strengthen the political as well as financial autonomy of Chinese lawyers, since the profit motive spurs them to defend their clients' rights with greater vigor.[71] With these changes, public demand for legal assistance has increased. In response, the 1996 Lawyer's Law, which privatized the bar, mandates that free legal aid be provided to the needy. In addition, university-based and other legal aid groups are beginning to mushroom in China.[72]

International attention to legal reform in authoritarian states tends to focus upon innovations that have the possibility of bringing the system into line with Western institutions and norms. The transformation of other elements of the state's legal and security apparatus often goes unnoticed. However, the reform of old guard institutions is as important as the introduction of new laws and structures. For example, during the Maoist era in China, work units and neighborhood committees were charged with monitoring citizens' activities and attitudes, and they assumed de facto judicial and police functions. Their responsibilities for political and social control have greatly diminished in the reform period. Some work units are still asked by local authorities to perform law enforcement functions, such as detaining employees. One measure of change is that they have reportedly refused.[73]

In strict authoritarian systems, the law serves a variety of purposes. Beyond the primary function of maintaining state control, it may provide cosmetic cover for authoritarian excesses or, in revolutionary periods, reflect the social engineering goals of the regime. When states begin to liberalize they add (but do not immediately remove) functions to the legal mix that act as nascent checks on the arbitrary use of authority and incipient protection of citizens' rights. During the early stages of reform, these new functions often run parallel to the others. Approaching the rule of law in these societies is a matter not of ousting old authoritarian practices and structures but of outdistancing them.

Elections and Other Mixed Signals

In the post–cold war era, democracy promoters caution one another against viewing elections as the sum total of the democratic process. Despite this, elections are rightly seen as landmarks in democratic development. Their use by authoritarian leaders is therefore perplexing to many Westerners. During the cold war, authoritarian regimes on both ends of the political spectrum relied upon elections, in which their own victory was a foregone conclusion, to enhance their international image. Right-wing authoritarians frequently resorted to "demonstration elections" to add democratic gloss after seizing power through nondemocratic means. Beyond the domestic legitimacy they were intended to convey, these exercises enabled the regime's democratic allies to justify to their own domestic populations a military partnership or economic assistance for the country. For this reason, Western nations themselves often suggested that authoritarian regimes organize ex post facto elections. One classic example was the "demonstration election" in South Vietnam, urged upon the regime in 1967 by the United States.[74] Marxist-Leninist governments also conducted show elections, in which only one candidate per post was allowed. Their aims were largely to counter Western charges that they had no popular legitimacy, but some leaders also believed that these rituals would bring their societies closer to the goal of "democratic centralism."

With ideological competition among nations abating, liberalizing authoritarian regimes are making ad hoc use of the electoral process for internal reasons. These exercises prompt Western observers to search for signs of democratic conversion within the regime. However, in the early stages of liberalization, leaders are more likely to take an instrumental approach to popular participation than an ideological one. For example, elections may be employed to secure support for the regime's continued rule by allowing limited contests at the national level among candidates restricted to regime members or regime-approved individuals.

A classic illustration of this was the 1997 presidential election in Iran, in which all candidates were members of the ruling clergy and were pre-selected by the Guardian Council. The pool of candidates was restricted by the constitutional requirement that leaders uphold the tenets of Shi'a Islam, effectively eliminating 11 percent of Iranians, and by the fact that women do not meet religious requirements for leadership. However, when the spectrum within a regime is widening, even limited elections have an element of uncertainty and risk an unpredictable outcome. Muhammad Khatami, an avowed moderate, probably survived the vetting process because he was considered a longshot by the regime. In his campaign, how-ever, he ran on an explicit platform of political reform and aggressively employed Western techniques, such as focus groups and bus tours. His vic-tory is largely attributed to his support among women and students. In the medium term, the progress of reform is often dependent upon whether such "upsets" are allowed to continue. The year 2000 parliamentary elec-tions in Iran are a watershed in this regard. The exuberant majority handed reform candidates demonstrates that Khatami's election cannot be con-sidered a fluke and, in some ways, may be more threatening to conserva-tives than the 1997 elections. But if the election results indicate a broad-based momentum for liberalization in Iran, they do not guarantee the continuation, or consolidation, of that trend. Although the presidency and the Parliament of Iran are presently in the hands of reformers, they are flanked by a greater number of institutions (the Guardian Council, secu-rity forces, broadcast media, and the judiciary) that are more influenced by conservatives.[75]

Beyond such restricted national contests, elections may also be used to strengthen the regime's popularity with certain segments of the population, with fire walls built into the process to prevent the spread of elected rule to other levels or groups. To maintain their image as populists, particularly in rural areas, leaders often permit local elections alone. In Bangladesh in the mid-1980s, for example, President Mohammad Ershad organized *upazilla* (county) elections at the height of martial law.

These controls negate the notion held by many Western democracy activists that popular participation is uncontainable once it is exercised in any form. On the other hand, they do not necessarily mean that electoral exercises in authoritarian states are not democratic on an individual basis or that they do not make a substantial contribution to political reform. In the long run, electoral experience is seldom wasted on a population. Among the new democracies of Africa, Asia, and Latin America are several that experienced a long succession of manipulated and flawed elections in authoritarian periods, during which lessons on the democratic process (or its absence) were learned—by citizens if not by the regime.

Rather, in authoritarian states, even liberalizing ones, elections are often less than the sum of their parts because of their strict limits and their instrumental use to the regime. Within this context, the cause célèbre of elections in authoritarian states, measured by the attention they receive in the international press, are village elections in China, which have now been held in a majority of Chinese villages.[76] These processes originated in the failure of the Mao regime to establish self-supporting commune systems in the rural areas of China and the general disarray of grassroots organizations after the Cultural Revolution. In this vacuum "villagers committees" were formed spontaneously during the late 1970s to provide basic needs and services that the fragmented system of local government could not. These new organizations were not perceived to threaten the central government. To the contrary, the regime accepted them as a new route to the party's long-standing goal of rural self-management, although villagers committees did not supplant the formal institutions of local rule. Since committees were required to obtain funds for projects from local revenue, expectations of support from the central government could be reduced in the countryside as a whole. These committees had a number of other, more subtle, benefits for the regime. Villagers committees could hold local government officials and local party cadres accountable for efficient government, a task made difficult for the regime by deteriorating relations between the central party and local branches. Moreover, the central government's public support of the new system helped maintain the rural population's loyalty to the party, however disillusioned they might be with local cadres.

Elected villagers committees have also been useful in helping implement certain central government policies, such as the one-child limit, which have proved to be unpopular.[77] Since villagers committees do not link up officially with other levels of government, demand for a bottom-up progression toward elected government can be contained. Indeed, as a measure of the central government's comfort with this process, foreign assistance for the development of villagers committee elections is encouraged and received from a variety of sources, ranging from the United Nations Development Programme, to the European Union, to private American foundations.[78]

There is no equivalent momentum for electoral reform at this time in Vietnam or Laos. However, within the strict confines of a party-controlled system of limited contests, some quiet signs of increased political participation are emerging. In elections for National Assembly deputies in Vietnam, the party has relaxed its one-seat–one-candidate rule and allows multiple candidates to compete for seats. Although most members of Parliament belong to the Communist Party, nonmembers are permitted to run provided they have passed the party's screening process. In 1997 elections the number of nonparty members of the Assembly rose to 15 percent, almost double that of the previous Congress.[79] Laos also permits nonparty candidates to run and now has one nonparty member in the National Assembly.[80] While such indications are mildly encouraging, it is possible to make too much of the presence of nonparty members in these contests, since some are persuaded to join the party after the election. Moreover, nonparty politicians in this context should not be equated automatically with an opposition-in-waiting, much less a de facto democratic front.

In many Middle Eastern states, electoral reform is not only a matter of moving a top-down or bottom-up strategy along but also of expanding the franchise across gender or other social lines. Political rights for women vary dramatically across the region, but in none of the remaining authoritarian states can women be said to enjoy full rights. The conservative tide of Islamic fundamentalism, combined with entrenched social custom, make rapid progress in this area unlikely. Political rights for women are as much a social issue as a political one, and in many societies social concerns override political progress. The paradox of a democratizing legislature in Kuwait overriding a traditional patriarch's request for greater political rights for women demonstrates the complexity of this problem. Improvement in this regard will likely move in tandem with greater educational and economic opportunity, trends that are emerging in several countries but at a very modest rate.[81]

Electoral reforms in authoritarian states create sharp debate among Westerners about the value of such experiments because of their obvious ambiguities. To some, the regime's motives in authorizing these steps, as well as the potential benefits for the leadership in renewed legitimacy, eclipse any gains in pluralism. Others are inclined to heed the unspoken acknowledgment in these reforms. Whatever short-term advantage may accrue to the regime in granting a small opening in the political system, the inevitable effect is a loosening of the political reins.

Many Westerners seeking to encourage political change in authoritarian societies look for reforms that represent a break from the past and presumably promise a more democratic future as a result. However, as the preceding discussion of change in the formal sectors of these states suggests, reforms are likely to be rooted more in continuity than in change. By the unspoken rules of liberalization, continuity permits these experiments to go forward, which may ultimately move the system toward greater openness.

3

Mothers and Mobile Phone Mobs: Renegotiating Civil Society

In the post–cold war period, Westerners who are disappointed by the lack of formal democracy in authoritarian states often place their hopes on civil society. High-profile demonstrations of "people power" in oppressed societies have resonance with Americans in particular. In the twentieth century, America's leading social movements—civil rights, environmental protection, consumer and women's rights—were rooted in the nongovernmental sector. By contrast, traditional forms of political participation, such as voting and party affiliation, have declined.[1] The American public is reported to be increasingly disillusioned with the ability of government to meet citizens' needs or solve social problems, as the looming crisis in Social Security funding demonstrates. This view of civil society as a catalyst, as well as a social and political avenger, is not without ideological contours. Inevitably, these assumptions permeate U.S. policies to promote political change in authoritarian societies.

Definitions of civil society vary in breadth and focus. At its broadest, civil society encompasses all groups and activities not legally bound to the state: the business community, religious organizations, political parties, media, local philanthropy, social service organizations, advocacy groups, and even organized crime. Individually or in combination, all of these may contribute to social pluralism and affect the relationship between state and society. Because authoritarian regimes almost always restrict or quell any organized political opposition, this study employs a narrow definition of civil society and focuses on nonpolitical voluntary groups in which some expansion, in both scope and autonomy, is possible during periods of liberalization. Indeed, the emergence of these nongovernmental organizations (NGOs) is often a sign of increasing social space. As liberalization progresses, they may assume some functions previously held by the state and may become significant players in public debate on reform and other policy issues. For this reason, although they are usually not overtly political, they may also help expand political space.

However, Western policymakers and democracy activists often gloss over, or ignore altogether, the phenomenon of apolitical NGOs in authoritarian systems. There are several reasons for this oversight. The first is a blank slate approach, or the assumption that associational life is alien to societies under authoritarian rule. In this view, regimes are immune to or refuse to tolerate all public pressure, and citizens lack any concept of social organization. Thus civil society can awaken only under democratization, most likely with a jump-start from the international community. Conversely, any obvious sign of an invigorated or agitated society—such as the Tiananmen Square movement in China in the late 1980s—is taken as an indication of impending democratization.

Nonetheless, all of the regions that presently have liberalizing authoritarian states have histories of civic organization and philanthropy. Although they may have been interrupted during periods of severe repression, these traditions have proved to be surprisingly durable. In times of relaxation, historical memory is often recalled to help revive associational life, albeit on different terms. Some forms of association were stimulated by religious requirements for merit-making (as in China and other societies with Buddhist influence), which eventually gave rise to charitable organizations. In traditional monarchies, private individuals or groups who hoped to strengthen their position with the ruling order often assumed responsibility for providing social services and formed trusts for this purpose. The shape of civil society may also reflect the influence of past colonization or other prolonged foreign contact, even in those states that have undergone revolutionary breaks from their political and social past. In Vietnam's south, for example, new social service networks and other forms of social activism are emerging that retain some characteristics of groups formed in the 1950s and 1960s with French and American assistance and training.[2]

During the early twentieth century, university-based and other intellectual groups in several of these countries agitated for social and political change. These were primarily modernist or anticolonial movements, which historians have since loosely translated as early democracy movements. One example was the Chinese New Culture Movement of 1915, based at Peking University.[3] Many new democracies have several such movements in their authoritarian pasts. In Thailand, the student revolution based at Thamasat University in 1973 was instrumental in overthrowing the military regime, although the military reclaimed its rule in 1976 and killed dozens of Thamasat students in the process. However, during the democratic period beginning in the late 1980s, many politicians and advisers to the government were Thamasat faculty and students from the 1970s. The Kwangju student demonstrations in South Korea, although not as influential as the Thai movement, also had impact on Korea's democratic development. In the late 1990s, former president Chun Doo Hwan, who had ordered the Kwangju massacre, was tried and convicted for the crime.

In gauging the impact of student and other intellectual movements on the development of civil society, it is important not to equate them automatically with grassroots or mass movements. History has shown that the success of intellectuals in promoting political change lies in their ability to forge coalitions with other social forces. Thus the Tiananmen Square movement in China ultimately failed not because of the crackdown in 1989 but because the students had not been able to develop widespread support at the grassroots level (although they did find some support among urban elements, and even within government ranks). On the other hand, student protesters in Indonesia in 1998 were able to press successfully for Suharto's resignation because their cause was taken up, and taken over, by populist Muslim associations.

The second ideological blinder is the view of civil society as a uniform and united good. Specifically, many Westerners assume the citizenry of an authoritarian state to be a monolithic, would-be liberal force, continually yearning for greater political freedom.[4] However, popular demand for change fluctuates in authoritarian societies, as it does in democratic ones. The Spanish citizenry in the 1950s, still recovering from the civil war, was lethargic in comparison to later periods of reform. After the Cultural Revolution in China, the student population, which Mao Tse-tung had harnessed to help purge the regime and broader society of "revisionists," was doggedly apolitical on the whole, although a small number joined the Democracy Wall movement of 1978–79.[5] Recent experience suggests that economic reform makes civil society only more complex, with wider political divisions. Although the rise of private enterprise in China has stimulated associational life and encouraged freedom in the print media, the business community itself is politically conservative in comparison to many other elements of Chinese society.[6] In Iran, the *bazaari* class is tied to conservative factions of the ruling clergy, which they believe better protect their interests.

A third assumption basic to the Western view of civil society is that state and society are inherently in conflict with one another. Civil society is often defined in terms of what it stands against;[7] in this view, cooperation with the state risks contaminating society. Political reform is therefore a zero-sum process, in which society becomes increasingly independent of the state but is also increasingly confrontational.

This view of state and society at total odds serves neither liberalization nor democratization. The dictates of authoritarian rule do not draw distinct lines between state and society. (In some societies, this is as much cultural as it is political. For example, in the Chinese language there is no generally accepted term for *civil society*, while there are multiple terms for *state*.)[8] On the contrary, in severe authoritarian systems (and, by definition, in totalitarian systems) regimes penetrate society in order to reshape it. Mass organizations function as "transmission belts" for ideology or simply for regime control. They mobilize the population and preempt powerful special interests, such as labor.[9] Although mass mobilization is most commonly associated with Marxist-Leninist regimes, it has figured in some right-wing authoritarian systems as well. Argentina under Juan Perón was one example. During the cold war, noncommunist regimes in Southeast Asia organized and oversaw mass organizations in rural areas, to counter the threat of communist insurgency.[10] The military government in Burma continues to operate a pseudo-civil society of mass organizations that, in theory, encompasses 20 percent of the adult population (since many government officials are compelled to join). These groups are legally classified as social organizations, but their primary function is political, to provide crowds of suitable size for pro-government rallies.[11]

Certainly, many civil society reformers in nations emerging from authoritarian rule aim to expand the space between state and society. However, with the lines between these two blurred, this work takes place not in an autonomous civil sector but in the gray areas between state and society. Nor should this approach necessarily be abandoned during the democratization period. At that point, civil society groups may unite in opposition to the regime. However, in those nations where there is a sharp break between state and society, as was the case in a number of Eastern European countries during the 1980s, new democratic leaders often find it difficult to govern. They face a political opposition that is concerned solely with overturning its opponents and a society that remains categorically opposed to all authority.

The work of civil society development in the liberalization process is not in rupturing relations between state and society but in recasting them. For a more active civil society to emerge, state and society must agree on new definitions of citizenship. In post-totalitarian systems, the initial step is in forging a concept of society as a collection of individual citizens rather than as an indivisible "mass." This has implications for the citizen's relationship not only to his fellow citizens but also to the state. For this reason, some civil society development must occur in the public sector. In China, for example, the establishment of a universal system of taxation has introduced the concept of citizens as taxpayers, with some means to hold government accountable for the use of public funds. In this realm, citizens are shifting from their role as servants of the party (and of the emperor during imperial times) to the "creditors" of government.[12]

The tactics of reform also encourage state and society to maintain links during political liberalization. As moderates emerge in the regime and the bureaucracy, their positions are strengthened if they can forge alliances with like-minded elements of civil society. In the mid-1980s, informal coalitions between civil society reformers and factions of the Philippine armed forces were crucial to the eventual victory of NAMFREL, which was due as much to military defections from the Marcos regime as to popular uprising. At that same time in China, reformers in the regime were strengthened by support from the intellectual community. It was only when reforms fell prey to corruption that intellectuals turned against the party in the late 1980s. Civil society pioneers also stand to benefit from links to the state during the early stages of political reform. Following the cardinal rule of the liberalization process, those reforms that meet with the regime's approval, even tacitly, are more likely to survive and ultimately to succeed.

Accidental Openness

In authoritarian systems, reforms in government are usually the result of intense deliberation and negotiation within the regime. Openings in civil society, on the other hand, are often unplanned and undeclared. Change in the formal sector proceeds at a cautious, incremental pace. In the civil sector, it is much more likely to move by opportunistic surges, although these may occur at intervals of several years. These surges may correspond to overt political change, as seen in Iran, or to economic reform, as is the case in China.

In some Leninist states in the post–cold war period, the opportunity for enlarging social space is found in the process of market reform. Economic liberalization reduces the role of the state and eventually shrinks the state as a whole.[13] As a result, governments find it necessary to privatize state welfare functions to some degree. This is an enormous undertaking in post-totalitarian systems. Major sectors such as housing and employment must be transferred to the market economy, and functions remaining with the state must be adjusted to lower funding levels. In China, the provision of social services, which remain the nominal responsibility of the government, is approached through various means. These include devolution to local government and community agencies, new fee-paying schemes, and relaxed rules on revenue-raising by state agencies.[14]

Beyond the growing privatization of large areas of social care and new arrangements for state-sponsored welfare, voluntary groups are being formed spontaneously in the Chinese population to provide social services.[15] These address a wide range of needs that citizens perceive to be underfunded or ignored by the state, ranging from care of the disabled, to environmental protection, to help for battered women.[16] The founders of these groups are often not professionals in the services they offer but ordinary citizens in need of technical, financial, or moral support from society: the mothers of autistic children, or homosexuals seeking information on health care.

The regime's official response to this phenomenon is one of ambivalence. All civil society organizations are in principle subject to financial and bureaucratic regulations in China, but these regulations have thus far failed to set clear boundaries. Regulatory confusion can be an aid to pluralism, and group founders have been able to find and make use of loopholes in the law. For example, some social service organizations that do not meet the bureaucratic requirements of a charity have been registered as business organizations without changing their basic structure or activities. Overall, an organization's ability to survive depends not on legal definitions but on the degree to which it is perceived to support the goals of the central government without threatening it. A second major criterion for survival is the ability to secure private funding, from foreign or domestic sources. Some civil society groups receive official stipends, but an increasing number must depend upon independent funding, from donors or through fee-paying arrangements. Even government-sponsored organizations are required to seek outside funding to extend their activities beyond the most basic functions.[17]

Another significant development in self-paying pluralism in China is the rapid privatization of mass media, particularly in the print sector, and a resulting leap in press freedom. This too is closely linked to market reform. During the early 1980s, cutbacks on state subsidies forced print publishers into the market. Book publishers were given de facto power to choose authors and subject matter, and privately produced books quickly overwhelmed their official competition. In 1979, the state-owned Xinhua media empire held 95 percent of the book publishing market; by 1988, it could attract only one-third of the market share.[18] During the 1990s and into the new century, semi-independent and nonlicensed publishers and distributors were increasingly able to circumvent government control of content. The cause of press freedom has been aided by the taste of the book-buying public and of the intelligentsia in particular. Controversial accounts of regime infighting, corruption, and the state of contemporary politics in China are automatic best-sellers.[19] The impact of this surge in book publishing, however, is often ignored in Western assessments of freedom in China. During the summer of 1999, after Chinese demonstrations against the bombing of the Chinese embassy in Belgrade, Western editorial writers were quick to claim that the Chinese people were unable to understand the motivations of the North Atlantic Treaty Organization (NATO) in the Kosovo intervention because of biased reporting in the state media. They were apparently unaware that during the early days of the intervention, no fewer than six Chinese-language titles had appeared in urban bookstalls, debating the Kosovo issue from a range of perspectives.

A similar shift has been seen in print journalism in China. By the mid-1980s, nonparty papers outnumbered party organs by a ratio of ten to one.[20] A noticeable side effect has been the decrease in propaganda content in the party papers. With its newfound gravity, the private print media has assumed investigative and muckraking functions. Like book publishers, newspaper editors have discovered that what is provocative and sensational sells, and exposés of official malfeasance have particular appeal.[21] As with the emergence of voluntary social service organizations, the regime's response to the surge in print media has been mixed. The party has made clear that it will not tolerate direct criticism of top leaders or official ideology, and journalists exercise self-censorship along those lines. However, the regime has also acknowledged a limited watchdog role for the media. In particular, it has quietly encouraged reporting on corruption in support of its own highly publicized anticorruption campaign.[22]

In relative terms, the most surprising expansion of press freedom in China has been in the electronic media, which is more easily controlled by government than print journalism in virtually all authoritarian systems. The costs of entry for electronic media are significantly higher than for print. Even here, however, the market is gaining ground. In order to maintain a critical mass of listeners and viewers (and to diminish their interest in foreign broadcasts), government radio and television stations have reduced packaged government programming. Featured instead are live news, call-in programs, and even interviews with celebrity intellectuals who were silenced after 1989, all of which are difficult to censor.[23] Although they remain under nominal government control, some stations and many programs are increasingly independent because they are able to attract revenue from commercials. Foreign broadcasts also draw a multilayered response from the government. The regime has no hesitation about jamming programs sponsored by foreign governments, particularly those with the avowed purpose of promoting freedom of expression in China. However, general news and entertainment ventures, such as commercial satellite television, receive more delicate handling. This is due in part to another reality of market reform: elements of the state are themselves invested in growth industries, including private media. In the mid-1980s, it was revealed that a growing number of local work units and party-sponsored block committees had set up mini cable networks for profit, including feeds from Star TV.[24]

In Iran, press licenses have been liberally granted since Khatami's election, but the new surge of newspapers and journals has been greeted with attempts at repression by the fundamentalist elements of the regime, who retain control over state censorship. This tug of war is exacerbated by the fact that new media has burgeoned on both ends of the political spectrum. While this is in theory a boon to pluralism, hard-liners are sometimes inclined to close progressive newspapers when they feel the conservative balance is in jeopardy, either in the regime or in the press. A complicating factor is that some Iranian newspapers are established as surrogate opposition parties, because press licenses are easier and safer to obtain than is official tolerance of a new party.[25]

Just as these elements of accidental openness may be difficult for the regime to control, so they are difficult for outsiders to assess. These privatizing sectors lack institutional infrastructure or laws to protect their present degree of freedom. Their status with the government is best measured not by laws on the books, which are sure to be repressive, but by the extent to which those laws are implemented (or ignored). Because their most spectacular growth occurs outside officially defined parameters, reliable statistics are difficult or impossible to obtain. Informal gains in pluralism may therefore be discounted in external assessments of political change, although they are never ignored by the ruling group.

GONGOs and Other Amphibians

No civil society can develop completely in an informal, haphazard way. To best serve the public interest, nongovernmental organizations must be able to carry out their functions in an orderly and sustained manner. To do so, they must operate in a civic environment that includes reliable sources of funding, mechanisms of self-regulation to promote competence and accountability, and a working relationship with the state, however arm's-length that might be. These conditions suggest not only a high level of autonomy for the civil sector but also a foundation of trust between state and society. In nations under authoritarian rule, these elements are distant goals. Movement toward them follows the larger pattern of liberalization: incremental change from the inside out, in which state attitudes are transformed at the same time that new groups and institutions gain influence. While civil society itself may surge upon occasion, developing a framework for the effective and regular operation of groups is a more plodding process.

It is necessary therefore to look not only at the few exemplary civil society organizations making strides in autonomy but also at the larger group of civic associations with links to the state. In civil society terminology, the latter groups are often referred to as *government-owned nongovernmental organizations,* or *GONGOs.*[26] This term is most frequently used for civil society groups in the Leninist states, although these groups are found in authoritarian systems in other regions. In traditional Middle Eastern societies, government-backed social groups are often referred to as *Royal NGOs* or *RANGOs.* Although designated as nongovernmental organizations, the boards of directors of RANGOs are usually appointed by royal decree, and the groups are charged with carrying out government-designed development projects.[27] As societies in this region become more pluralistic, however, a broader spectrum of nongovernmental organizations in emerging. In Kuwait, for example, some of the most vigorous NGOs are technically illegal—that is, not registered—but are able to operate with increasing freedom. Many of these unauthorized groups, some of which monitor public spending or advocate stronger protection of human rights, work closely and openly with parliamentary committees.[28]

In Iran, the giant *bunyad*s, or assistance foundations, are closely tied to the ruling clergy and as a result effectively function as state organs. Some foundations administer funds seized from the shah after the 1979 revolution. Their aggregate wealth enables them to exercise virtual monopolies over the financial, housing, transport, and agricultural sectors.[29] Since Islamic custom provides for clergy-determined social projects and organizations, the relationship between the state and the *bunyad*s is an important glue in the maintenance of Islamic rule in Iran. Reformists tend to view the *bunyad* in an increasingly negative light because of their lack of accountability and call for for privatization or nationalization of their assets. They maintain that the size of the *bunyad* holdings maintains a dangerous gray zone of economic activity that undermines legal enterprise in Iran and maintains a powerful instrument in the hands of the conservative clergy. More fundamentally, the network of *bunyad*s underscores the overall weakness of the legal framework for both politics and business in Iran.[30] Whether further liberalization would change the nature of the *bunyad*s or create a core of civil society organizations of a more secular character remains to be seen.

To Western sensibilities, which assume the boundary between state and society to be clear and immutable, GONGOs and their variations are a contradiction in terms. In reality, the great majority of social organizations in authoritarian systems are encompassed within the orbit of state power and are likely to remain there during the liberalization period, although they move farther away from the center as reform progresses.

Many formal curbs on nongovernmental activity are inscribed in regulations on civil society organizations. Typically, authoritarian governments require that NGOs be paired with state ministries and obtain approval from those agencies for significant steps, such as the acceptance of funds from foreign donors. A number of links lie outside the formal system and are more difficult to detect. The broad web of personal ties in authoritarian systems is usually replicated in state-society relations. Thus an NGO may have on its board of directors several "retired" regime officials, as is the case with the Iranian *bunyad*s, a circumstance likely to continue for some time, given the large funds these foundations have at their disposal.[31]

Despite these obvious constraints, an increasing number of NGOs in liberalizing states depart in spirit and function from the "caged sector" of mass organizations that make up the societal base in severe authoritarian rule. The distinctions between these groups and old-style mass organizations, which also continue to operate during liberalization, are increasingly apparent. While civil society organizations remain under some remnant of government control, they become less subject to government direction in the selection and conduct of activities. In strict authoritarian systems, the state sets the agenda of the civil society organization. In liberalizing systems, NGOs increasingly set their own agendas, with varying reactions from the state.

In China, agenda greatly influences the degree of autonomy granted to a civil society organization by the regime. Recent research indicates that associations with clear, narrowly defined missions that support economic development goals (such as energy efficiency) enjoy the greatest independence. Groups that represent large segments of the population (such as women) may encounter the most difficulty carving out space. On a different axis, however, organizations that provide relief or other basic services are allowed more independence than many policy study or advocacy groups.[32] Thus an organization providing relief to indigent women may be more acceptable than a policy study group that takes issue with official economic policy. Although the regime's self-protective reflexes are evident on this grid, so is a pragmatic approach to social pluralism. At this juncture in China's reform, the most successful NGOs are likely to be the most amphibious ones, serving the broad policy goals of the government while pushing the edge of autonomy.

When the state and nongovernmental organizations agree upon goals, NGO roles can expand dramatically. For example, in the floods along the Yangtze River in China in 1998, civil society organizations played a pivotal role in delivering assistance, relocating citizens to safe areas, and addressing other immediate needs (such as organizing makeshift schools for children). Beyond these functions, NGOs broke new ground in two directions in the aftermath of the floods. They served as major fundraisers, securing roughly U.S. $2 million for flood relief in less than two months. Equally important, they acted as coordinators among government agencies, private companies, and volunteers to deliver funds and materials to affected areas, a mobilizing function that had been the sole responsibility of the state.[33]

As the nongovernmental sector becomes more active in liberalizing societies, official mass organizations are often compelled to change as well. Although governments may take steps to protect these institutions and preserve their close ties to the state, they are seldom able to maintain their budgets at past levels. Losing comprehensive life-support systems, these organizations are forced to reconsider their roles and become more responsive to their clientele in civil society.[34]

Westerners are largely intolerant of the GONGO syndrome in liberalizing authoritarian states because they are inclined to focus more on form than on function. They also tend to ignore the full range of relations between state and society in their own systems. In the United States, the government relies heavily upon the nonprofit sector to pursue domestic goals and even foreign policy goals; NGOs are rewarded accordingly. Government funding of the nonprofit sector now outdistances private philanthropy at a rate of two to one.[35] The structure and operation of American civic organizations are also influenced by the requirements for tax-exempt status placed upon NGOs under Section 501(c)(3) of the Internal Revenue Code. These restrictions are generally mild but they do, for example, prohibit tax-exempt NGOs from attempting to influence legislation.[36]

Also interesting is the rise of *quasi-nongovernmental organizations*, or *QUANGOs*, in a number of Western societies, including the United States, France, Germany, and the United Kingdom. These organizations are prominent in foreign policy, where there is often tension between several immediate policy objectives or between short- and long-term goals. QUANGOs can pursue policy-related objectives (such as democracy promotion or conflict resolution) with more singularity of purpose than governments, avoiding the trade-offs that dilute or skew official policy. They engage in dialogue with their governments on overall policy goals but maintain autonomy in their selection of board officials, their daily operations, and their individual program activities. To enable them to serve long-term national interests, they receive sustained core funding from the government, often directly from the legislature or from an agency "pass-through." This model has endured because neither the government nor the QUANGO views the partnership between the two as compromising the independence of the QUANGO.[37]

Few would argue that high levels of government funding of NGOs, special arrangements like the QUANGO model, or the tax conditions on civil groups constitute an assault on the autonomy of Western civil society. These factors do suggest that state-society relations require a multidimensional perspective and that civil society organizations are defined as much by their cooperation with the state as by their distance from it.

Approaching Advocacy

It is a given in rigid authoritarian systems that social groups participate in the policy process not by their own direct representation but through officially designated bureaucracies, if indeed they participate at all. As these systems relax and as civil society becomes more assertive, the impetus for civil groups to take on some advocacy functions becomes stronger. Governments are predictably more wary of nongovernmental organizations participating in the policy process in this way, however tangentially, than they are of using NGOs as conduits for social services. However, a regime may tolerate citizens' advocacy when it contributes to the solution of social problems the government finds difficult to control. This is particularly true in societies in the midst of market reform, where a breakneck pace of economic change creates new issues—such as environmental protection and consumer rights—that fall outside the traditional experience of the regime. Thus even citizens' participation in public affairs, which may Westerners view as a hallmark of democratization, can pass the dual-purpose test of liberalization.

Not surprisingly, the issue areas allowed more citizens' advocacy are those that stay well away from narrow political interests. This strategy of putting social instrumentality ahead of political ideology has proved successful in a number of liberalizing states. One reason is that the regime is seldom the sole object of such activism: local authorities, against whom the regime may also have complaints, and private corporations are often targeted as well. In Taiwan during the late 1970s and early 1980s, groups dedicated to environmental protection, women's welfare, and consumer rights were better able to pressure the government on policy issues than opposition parties, which were outlawed at the time. Some, such as the Consumers Foundation, were aggressive in petitioning the government and organized mass demonstrations without reprisal.[38] In South Africa during the early stages of emergence from apartheid, the first black civil society organizations were housewives collectives and educational foundations. Avowed anti-apartheid groups, many of which were in exile outside South Africa's borders, are better seen in the context of political insurgency and later political party development than in the growth of citizens' advocacy.[39]

A similar pattern of social instrumentality is emerging in China. Although access to government channels is quite restricted for civil society organizations in comparison to the situation in democratizing states, new pathways are emerging on an issue-specific basis. For example, the National People's Congress has consulted with prominent women's hotline groups, which have a hands-on feel for contemporary family issues, on a new draft marriage law. In a more complicated interaction, conservation groups in a locality recently appealed to a leading Beijing-based environmental advocacy organization for help in halting damage to wildlife by local authorities in a regional development project. The Beijing group subsequently petitioned a central government official, who in turn pressured the local authorities to cease those activities that were directly harming wildlife.[40]

Not every lobbying effort is as effective as the wildlife conservation coup. At this stage of China's civil society development, there are few such clear, bottom-line results. The better measures of progress at this time are the linkages formed among groups, both within society and between state and society, that carry the promise of a more dense and effective social sector. As liberalization progresses, these ties expand and begin to converge. In China, points of contact are growing between legislatures and NGOs, between the media and legislatures, and between NGOs and the media. Within issues areas, broad-based networks of civil society organizations are forming, giving urban groups some penetration to the grassroots and local groups a greater voice in framing national social issues.

Much of the civil society development described in this chapter contributes to social pluralism in liberalizing authoritarian states. However, the links between social and political pluralism are seldom straightforward or obvious. Strong, self-reliant civic organizations are a boon to political pluralism, but they do not automatically lead to it. Nevertheless, many Westerners leap to make that connection. In established democracies, a robust civil society provides the "social capital" necessary for healthy democratic institutions. In the post–cold war period, a new strain of literature on civil society in the advanced democracies has appeared.[41] These works revisit Tocqueville's theory that apolitical associations crossing major lines of conflict within a society (on racial issues, for example) provide the scaffolding required for democratic governance. Some therefore assume a developed civil society to be synonymous with a political democracy. However, simultaneous functions in advanced democracies do not necessarily mean that these functions emerged simultaneously in a nation's political history.

In many authoritarian states, a sequence in which social pluralism precedes political pluralism is more likely, but this is a loose generalization, more applicable to the Asian Leninist states than to some Middle Eastern ones. In traditional Arab nations, the reverse may in fact be true. An active, inclusive civil society may be more threatening to the regime than a liberalizing (but still controlled) political system. In the liberalization period, the formal political process can usually be manipulated to maintain the regime's bottom-line control. However, civil society development may mean breaking centuries-old traditions, such as those governing the roles of women, or opening the door to greater influence of fundamentalist groups.[42]

To be sure, in societies governed by brittle, personal regimes where there is little possibility of an evolution toward openness, social groups often assume political roles at the first opportunity. These groups may in fact have been established with clear political aims. The NAMFREL movement in the Philippines was a broad coalition of business, religious, and social groups, but it was formed with the intention of acting as a surrogate political party.[43] In states where authoritarian rule is more institutionalized, the regime is better able to enforce a separation between social and political development, if only for a time. In these societies, civic advocacy groups can at best provide a corridor between social and political pluralism that may widen as the liberalization process moves forward.

Going Global

Many of the social causes around which civil society groups are formed in authoritarian societies, such as environmental protection and women's rights, are also transnational issues that figure heavily in international debate. These issues are the focus of an emerging global polity, comprising inter-governmental agencies, nongovernmental organizations with regional or global reach, and a growing web of international covenants and protocols. But despite predictions at the end of the cold war that globalization would supplant the fraying system of nation-states, the sum of these institutions and processes has not outstripped the regulatory force of national governments, although some sectors (such as international trade) appear to coalesce on a global level more easily than others. Ironically, globalization has demon-strated a greater potential to promote change within individual societies. Authoritarian regimes usually have a knee-jerk aversion to unfiltered inter-national influence. Despite this, only those which are willing to forego the benefits of modernization (which includes technological advance) and full partnership in the international community are able to quarantine their soci-eties from global associational trends, although they are able to limit contact.

The transnational social movements of the post–cold war era (the major ones being environmental protection, population control, women's rights, and human rights) are encompassed in the popular conception of a global civil society.[44] The convening events for these movements have been global conferences, many of them under the aegis of the United Nations. As the decade has progressed, the role of nongovernmental organizations at these conferences has strengthened.

When they are acting en bloc, NGOs can function effectively as advocates and negotiators at international events. At the Earth Summit in Rio de Janeiro in 1992, the agreement to control greenhouse gases was largely the work of environmental NGOs, which proposed most of its structure and content and mobilized public pressure for its approval.[45] At the United Nations World Conference on Human Rights in Vienna in 1993, several Asian NGOs joined ranks publicly against their governments in support of a resolution to affirm the universality of human rights.[46] Other international and regional organizations have followed suit and opened their summits and conferences to NGOs, as interlocutors if not as full participants. International meetings that were once the exclusive purview of governments now resemble track-two exercises, in which the views of both official and non-governmental groups are aired if not integrated. Indeed, this paradigm is so pervasive that when governments do not open a second channel in international meetings (and when NGOs are not sufficiently coordinated among themselves), the meeting can be seriously disrupted, as was the 1999 World Trade Organization meeting in Seattle.

The effect of this more open international discourse on authoritarian nations is twofold. First, a subliminal message about the changing nature of international legitimacy is conveyed, since a country's image at these meetings depends in part on its providing NGO as well as government representation. Undoubtedly, many regimes reach into the "caged sector" of mass organizations for these events and are able to stage-manage their national NGO participation. But even mass organizations may benefit from the second effect, which is contact with a wide range of civil society organizations and demonstrations of nongovernmental advocacy.

This demonstration effect is greatest when authoritarian nations themselves host these international events. Western NGOs often oppose an international organization's decision to meet in a country whose civil society is not up to the standard of an established democracy. They maintain that the regime's legitimacy is enhanced when such events are held on their soil and that the occasion inspires the government to erect a Potemkin village of state-controlled organizations that they attempt to pass off as a nongovernmental sector.

This may be the case, but these arguments miss the larger point—the exponential benefit such events can have on the country's own civil society. The impact of an out-of-country meeting is more easily controlled, because frequently only approved NGOs attend from authoritarian countries. In-country events bring a wider spectrum of local civil groups and media in contact with their counterparts from more open societies. Western participants criticized the Chinese government for its attempts to control nongovernmental activity during the 1995 United Nations World Conference of Women in Beijing, with reason. However, the aftereffects of the conference in China, which have gone largely unnoticed by the West, are striking. Chinese observers report that many new women's NGOs were established in the wake of the conference, such as crisis hotlines, university-based women's studies centers, and legal aid groups. They rate these postconference organizations as more autonomous than other Chinese NGOs.[47] Some also credit the Women's Conference with bringing the term *nongovernmental organization* into the Chinese popular lexicon.

The Technical Edge

The post–cold war phenomenon of greatest potential for the development of civil society in many authoritarian systems is the arrival of advanced telecommunications. Low economic levels and government resistance have contained the spread of these technologies in many Middle Eastern and Asian Leninist states, and these conditions still apply to a considerable degree. However, in recent years their introduction into these societies has added a new dimension to the prospects for political change.

For more than a century, modernists have mythologized communications technology as a transformational force. Victorians were no less awed by the potential impact of the telegraph on society than post–cold war citizens are by the Internet.[48] By the second half of the twentieth century, the political uses of mass communications were apparent. Radio had emerged as a tool of mass propaganda in the Second World War. Throughout the cold war, the United States in particular relied upon broadcast radio (Radio Free Europe, Radio Liberty) as an ideological weapon against the Communist bloc. The world was reminded again of radio's potency in the 1990s, when "hate radio" was effectively employed to incite genocide in Rwanda. Television has been used by a wide range of democratic and authoritarian rulers to craft images of leadership that invariably depart from reality. Defense departments in advanced democracies are well aware that every war is a "television war" and that public support for military intervention will be affected more by what citizens see on their living room screens than by the best-crafted official speech.

With the near-religious regard for technology in the modern world, it is tempting to overstate its reach and power. Yet in 1998 only 100 million people in the world were estimated to have access to the Internet, and three-quarters of the world's population lacked even a telephone, much less a computer and modem.[49] However, for liberalizing societies the significance of technology is not only in its potential breadth but also in its changing nature. For most of the twentieth century, communications that have linked populations in authoritarian countries to the outside world, or to their own leaders, have been unilateral. Messages and information came from the outside in, or from the regime to the people. Post–cold war communications technology is increasingly reciprocal. Information now has the potential to flow out of, as well as into, these societies. Equally important, the means for citizens to communicate with one another are enhanced.

These new channels of communication within liberalizing nations have unmistakable implications for organizing civil society and for citizens' relations with the state. The most dramatic incidents of popular resistance against regimes in the past decade have been spurred by technology. During the Tiananmen Square demonstrations in 1989, Chinese dissidents communicated with one another and with the outside world by fax. In Bangkok in 1992, members of the Thai professional classes—dubbed "mobile phone mobs" for their passionate attachment to personal technology—coordinated antimilitary demonstrations with student leaders and with one another by cellular phone. In Indonesia in 1998, anti-Suharto resistance was coordinated by way of the Internet.

The greater potential for technology to strengthen civil society inheres not in these political flashpoints but in the everyday intercourse of civil and political life. In authoritarian societies with even limited access to the Internet, technology's use differs from the expansion of print and electronic media because there is no foundation of government-dominated organs for the regime to call upon as a counterweight. From its inception, the Internet has been a freer form of communication than any other in the country, at least to those few who can obtain it. In authoritarian states that are modernizing, the regime may be caught between the desire to expand the use of technology for economic reasons while attempting to curb citizens' use for social and political purposes. It is increasingly difficult to enforce a separation between these two. In China, for example, an ambitious plan to build a national computerized information infrastructure has caused the telecommunications industry to grow at an annual rate of 30 to 50 percent since 1989.[50] At the same time, the government requires that all Internet users register, is investing in technology to filter cyber-communications, and has promulgated regulations on acceptable topics for discussion. Chinese Internet users have discovered, however, that many of these restrictions can be circumvented by the use of proxy servers. Internet users constitute a very small percentage of the Chinese population—only 7 million at present—but they are concentrated in the educated classes and are increasing rapidly. From

1997 to 1998, their number rose by 75 percent,[51] and in 1999 the number of online users tripled.[52]

As the Internet has gradually spread among China's professional classes, the nature of discourse has also expanded, even on political issues. When political debate was first initiated on the web in China, it was a small-group, clandestine activity that resembled the *samizdat* publications of anti-Soviet dissidents in Eastern Europe during the later years of the cold war. The venues for this discussion were the websites of Western activist groups or Chinese dissidents in exile. More recently, Chinese service providers report that users are accessing a greater proportion of Chinese (rather than foreign) websites, many of which focus on a broad range of public issues.[53] Those few Chinese Internet magazines with specific political focus have also expanded their approach and their readership, occasionally airing the views of pro-reform government officials as well as private government critics.[54] At this juncture, the critical factor is not how strident the debate can be but how inclusive. These developments suggest that the Internet has the potential to serve as an instrument of indigenous debate in China rather than merely a narrow tool of dissent. However, the rate at which Internet use develops will depend on factors outside the technological realm—in particular, economic growth that expands citizens' access to technology, as well as a more relaxed political environment.

It is easy to make too optimistic an assessment of the effects of technology in China and in several other authoritarian states at this time. Indeed, representatives of American business and some American legislators are couching China's imminent entry into the World Trade Organization as a move that will allow political freedom in China to surge. In their view, it will unleash the Internet by giving foreign telecommunications companies parity with China Telecom, the government monopoly. There are several qualifications, both economic and political, to this theory that make it much less of a quick fix to China's political problems. Nevertheless, in countries where conditions favor the rapid growth of technology, the greater advantage is likely to go to society in the end, although it may alternate between the regime and society for several years.

In many other authoritarian states, the level of Internet use (and the absence of rapid economic growth) have not brought state and society to such reckoning. The nations of the Persian Gulf have been among the slowest to join the Internet community. Beyond the concern with political upheaval common to authoritarian governments worldwide, Gulf regimes fear that the Internet will also act as a conduit for westernization. The uneven growth of its use in the Gulf closely parallels the spectrum of political openness in the region. The populations of Iran and Kuwait rank as the most active users, with the others at some distance behind. Saudi Arabia, for example, has been linked to the Internet for several years, but public access is severely limited.[55]

This chapter and the preceding one paint what some may consider to be too positive a picture of political change in these "intransigent" authoritarian states. Without question, the short-term outlook for each of them favors the continuation of authoritarian rule in some form. Moreover, both regime behavior and civil society development in these states suggest that political liberalization will, in the near term, continue to be led by the regime, although there are tangible prospects for strengthening civil society in many cases. The early stages of political liberalization rarely produce clear-cut victories for the forces of freedom, but they can offer a surprising range of gains for pluralism in both state and society. The major questions of political control are seldom settled in the liberalization process. During this period, the task is to keep these questions open.

4

Radicals and Radios:
The U.S. Response to Authoritarian Regimes

The present policies of the United States that attempt to promote political change in authoritarian countries tend to reflect neither the nature nor the process of liberalization. Rather, they mirror the assumptions of many Americans about political transitions at the end of the cold war, as well as the role of the United States in the collapse of Soviet communist rule. These beliefs are so entrenched in some quarters of the policy community and the public that they are applied to the remaining authoritarian regimes by reflex. If certain initiatives "worked" with Moscow (and, by definition, the end of the cold war vindicated every policy move, however modest), then they are worth repeating in Beijing. To respond to these arguments, it is not sufficient to point out the differences between the present group of "hold-out" countries and the Eastern bloc nations or the cold war clients of the United States in Latin America and Asia. It is necessary as well to measure these notions of the cold war's end against the fuller reality of that time.

In the conventional wisdom of the 1990s, persisting into the present decade, the central article of faith is that the cold war was an ideological struggle and that its end was an orchestrated victory for democracy. No plainer statement of this view can be found than in the 1991 Report of the President's Task Force on Government International Broadcasting: "The Cold War was a contest of ideas. Our side won." This was the spontaneous anthem of political neoconservatives, editorial writers and officers of newly minted democracy promotion organizations after the collapse of the Soviet Union.[1] Throughout the 1980s, this group had subscribed to a singular vision of the Eastern bloc as an ideological entity, albeit one held together by military muscle and governed by regimes whose characters would not change up to the moment of collapse.

In this paradigm, the internal architects of political reform were the small groups of dissenters in each society who held ideological positions that corresponded to those of Western conservatives and intellectuals. Groups of dissidents in Eastern Europe, who did double-duty as democrats and independence leaders, were the most highly acclaimed. These groups did indeed have impact as their ideas filtered slowly into the thinking of political figures on the margins of the party nomenklatura.[2] In a few Eastern European countries, most notably Czechoslovakia, they provided the first post-Soviet leaders. However, this view greatly discounts moderates in official sectors who also sought to move their societies away from strict Marxist-Leninist tenets. Poland doubtless owes some of its new freedom to the Solidarity movement, but it is also indebted to the government officials who made concessions to openness in the Round Table Negotiations of the late 1980s. But an emphasis on dissidents, who were assumed to be roundly pro-Western, preserved the political framework of East and West as polar opposites. Giving weight in the equation of political change to communist reformers raised the possibility of ideological convergence at worst or, more likely, the existence of an unappealing gray middle ground.

Support for the dissident approach was bolstered in the United States by the slow-growing but high-profile human rights movement. During the last decade of the cold war, human rights groups clashed with political conservatives over anticommunist policy in Central America. However, there was greater commonality with regard to the Eastern bloc, since neither the government nor private groups had significant access or leverage in the internal affairs of these countries.

The ideological glue in this liberal-conservative alliance, which endures to the present day and provides the main support for idealpolitik in U.S. foreign policy, was the American belief in the sanctity of the individual. In Western political thought, particularly its American branch, civil and political rights are conferred upon citizens in their capacity as individuals. The individual is therefore taken to represent society as a whole. Individual rights play a central role in human rights policy as a whole. To pressure governments to improve their record on rights, activists seek to personalize policy by casting a spotlight on the most oppressed individuals and groups, who are often political dissidents and ethnic minorities. They are also inclined to focus on dissidents because doing so supports the belief that external actors can serve as surrogate watchdogs in countries where indigenous capacity to defend rights is weak or nonexistent. The best hope of doing this is with high-profile resisters who can capture international attention. However, such sponsorship is no guarantee either of improved rights or of dissidents' safety.

This practice first appeared in U.S. government policy in the administration of President Jimmy Carter during the late 1970s. Carter astonished Soviet president Leonid Brezhnev at their first official meeting in 1977 by presenting him with a list of Soviet dissidents whom the United States demanded be released from prison. In time, the briefcases of most high-ranking U.S. diplomats on official missions abroad held "the list" of individuals about whom Washington was concerned. Relations between the government and human rights groups improved as they exchanged information on the conditions of various dissidents, many of whom were political prisoners.

As the Eastern bloc moved closer to reform and, as it turned out, dissolution, the significance of its dissidents expanded in the West. They came to represent not only the rights denied to citizens in an oppressed society but the political will of the citizenry as a whole. This freedom-first approach, often identified by certain key verbs—populations are typically "clamoring" or "yearning" for political freedom, never rationally assessing their options— was too narrow an interpretation of a broad and complicated phenomenon in the Eastern bloc. Certainly, during the late 1980s these populations widely and publicly repudiated communist rule. However, it is far from clear that what attracted them to the Western way of life were the abstract liberal ideals of American democracy. Equal if not greater evidence suggests that citizens were rejecting Bolshevik austerity for the "bourgeois decadence" of the West, the very aspects of popular culture and consumerism that American conservatives deplored.[3] While American ideologues were cloaking Soviet citizens in the ideals of Thomas Jefferson, a visible percentage of Soviets appeared to be focusing on Madonna. Ideology, in the former Eastern bloc as elsewhere in the world, was tempered with a large dose of instrumentality.

These more variegated motives for political change were reflected throughout the 1990s in the mixed results of the democratic revolutions in these countries. Simultaneous transitions toward democracy and market economies proved to be more difficult than postcommunist leaders, or their Western supporters, had anticipated. Democracy often failed to deliver instant economic prosperity and opened the door to new social problems. Strains of authoritarianism, including reform communism, reemerged in second-round elections or in leaders who had previously sworn allegiance to democracy.

This uneven scorecard in the former Eastern bloc has not changed mainstream U.S. policy thinking about transitions out of authoritarian rule (although policymakers have adopted a more complicated view of consolidating democratic transitions once they have begun). Americans find it difficult to let go of their view of the cold war's end because of its companion belief that victory was due in large measure to the ideological resolve and the political exertions of the United States. Few attempts have been made to distinguish between the domestic factors that caused Soviet communism to unravel and the external forces that may well have influenced the timing and intensity of the process.[4] The perception of a grand sweep for the West removed the need to sort out success stories from failures in American foreign policy. All measures aimed at the Eastern bloc were accorded equal success, and none was too small to have weight. Thus rhetorical flourishes, such as Ronald Reagan's exhortation to Mikhail Gorbachev to "Tear down this [Berlin] wall" were elevated to the status of major policy moves. Many Americans also adopted the notion of unequivocable success in the Eastern bloc as a relief from the cynicism that grew out of attempts to effect political change in right-wing authoritarian allies. An arms-length confrontational relationship, they believed, was more effective than a close, cooperative one. It was also less of a moral compromise. This view therefore tended to ignore exchange programs, both official and private, and other links between Western and Eastern bloc societies that proliferated during the final years of the cold war.

This chapter delineates the ways in which this paradigm of the cold war's end has been translated into initiatives in American policy toward the countries that form the focus of this study. This model is applied unevenly across the range of target authoritarian states. It is most closely followed with the Asian Leninist states (and with Cuba), where it is deemed to be the most transferable, since the view of communism as a monolith lingers in both official and public views of these states.[5] It is also applied to right-wing totalitarian regimes (Burma and Iraq, for example) that show few if any signs of political liberalization at this time. This model is seldom employed in policies toward traditional Middle Eastern countries that are security allies or vital trading partners of the United States, but it does influence U.S. policy toward Iran.

The elements of this strategy are remarkably similar to cold war constructs. Public condemnation of repressive regimes is coupled with support (moral or financial) to groups that articulate Western democratic values, whether they are in-country or in exile. General populations are targeted through mass communications, usually international radio broadcasts. Just as these mechanisms are transferred from the cold war, so was the psychology of ideological warfare. One element of this is an ever-present sense of urgency and an exaggeration of the importance of individual events. An opponent regime is just one dissident arrest away from a total crackdown or one demonstration away from collapse. But the most significant carryover from the end-of-cold-war syndrome is the belief that one country can change the political direction of another if it is determined enough to do so. Thus authoritarian rule endures in China because the American body politic has not mustered sufficient political will to expunge it.

As these tactics are grafted onto post–cold war situations, there are of course nuances and modifications. For example, public criticism is now considered to be more effective if it is multilateral. But there are also significant differences between the cold war environment and the present one that cast doubt on the efficacy of this framework. The ideological purpose that brought its own order to American foreign policy in the cold war has dissolved for the most part. During the cold war, policymakers and the American public discovered how difficult and costly it can be to try to force democratization according to an external timetable on right-wing allies, even in the smallest states. In today's more fractious political environment, ambitious policies to micromanage internal change in another country are not likely to be launched, much less sustained. Those measures are generally reserved for extreme situations, such as failed states emerging from severe internal conflict. Instead, these carryovers from the cold war are employed in a piecemeal and haphazard fashion, more as symbols than as elements of a coherent strategy.

The Dissident Model

As detailed in previous chapters, the political liberalization process in train in a number of authoritarian countries walks a delicate line. Social and political space may be enlarged if it does not result immediately in organized opposition to the incumbent regime. In contrast, many of the policy measures that the United States applies to encourage freedom in these countries take frontal, openly political positions. Policymakers and assistance donors who subscribe to a strict ideological framework consider the most valuable activities to be those that openly call for democratic change and, directly or indirectly, for the downfall of the regime.

Many of these efforts are based outside the target country, often in democratic countries where they can be organized without obstruction or reprisal. They are frequently implemented by political exiles from the country who are assumed *in toto* to be an opposition, although these wide-ranging collections of individuals seldom resemble or operate as genuine opposition parties.

In some cases, an opposition that has never held power may be treated by Western policymakers as though it were a government-in-exile (as opposed to exiled leaders, such as Haiti's Jean-Bertrand Aristide, who were driven out of power by coup). This may occur in tandem with continued recognition of the incumbent government. For example, the U.S. government continues to recognize the military regime in Burma (although diplomatic representation to Rangoon was reduced after 1990), while the U.S. Congress appropriates funds to "the legitimate government of Burma," which it defines as the opposition.[6] Western politicians and activists are also prone to viewing exiled opposition figures as shadow leaders awaiting the collapse of a regime from afar, even if they had no actual claim to political power before leaving their home countries.

The tradition of offshore opposition is no mere American conceit. It is rooted in the history of much of the twentieth century and has served political forces across the spectrum. Sun Yat-sen, widely recognized as the father of modern China, spent several decades abroad planning his revolution. A pantheon of Asian communists—Zhou Enlai, Deng Xiaoping, Ho Chi Minh, and even members of Cambodia's Khmer Rouge—spent extensive periods studying and working abroad, preparing for revolution. (The notable exception was Mao Tse-tung).[7] In contrast to the more overt conquests that gave the Soviet Union control of Eastern Europe, the spread of communism in the developing world was a matter of military and political insurgency, often operating from bases in neighboring countries. Throughout the cold war the West made use of offshore opposition as well, to battle communist-led governments. These ranged from the ill-fated Bay of Pigs incident in Cuba in 1961 to support for the three-party Cambodian resistance, established on the Thai-Cambodian border in the 1980s, in opposition to a Vietnamese-installed government in Phnom Penh.[8]

However, with the end of the cold war, the power of the long-distance leader has declined. Western governments may give refuge to people persecuted for their political activities, but they are no longer likely to provide them with the major support needed to establish alternative polities. When the Cambodian opposition parties decamped to Thailand after the 1998 elections, which they considered to have been fraudulent, they met with apathy from the West. Their former patrons were not interested in providing open-ended life support to a disorganized opposition or in restarting an insurgency effort. There are a few exceptions to this rule. Present U.S. policy toward Iraq includes the possibility of both political and military support for an opposition, but the levels of funding would hardly support a major offensive.

Instead, post–cold war support for opposition groups in exile is better viewed as a moral boost than as an attempt to provide a critical level of assistance. This support usually takes the form of funds to small nonprofit organizations headed and staffed by dissidents. These groups seek to publicize political conditions in their home countries and often produce modest publications that are circulated among Western governments, advocacy groups, and exile communities. Although these organizations usually attempt to get information back into their home countries (and sometimes claim to be creating underground networks), on balance their constituencies lie outside the country.

Cold war financial support was often given directly to an opposition group by the U.S. government (and often included "advisory" services), but most current U.S. government aid to dissident exile groups is funneled through American nongovernmental organizations. The annual congressional earmark of funds to strengthen the Burmese opposition, which has expanded from $2 million in 1996 to $6 million in 2000, is administered primarily by the National Endowment for Democracy.[9] Some individual dissidents receive private funding from Western human rights groups or from universities, where they are often given institutional bases.

These types of offshore activities might be described, in a particular post–cold war twist, as "overt-covert." They aim to operate clandestinely in the target country but are publicized outside of the country, by the group or by its Western funders.[10] Although some projects support political organizing activities, such as training for "political defiance committees" of exiled Burmese students on the Thai-Burmese border,[11] the majority are information-related.

Assistance to exiled opposition figures and other political refugees has obvious merit on humanitarian grounds. Such individuals can also give policymakers first-hand information about conditions in authoritarian countries at the time of their departure. Indeed, émigré groups, ranging from Cubans fleeing Fidel Castro in the 1960s to Chinese students after the Tiananmen Square crackdown, often have a measurable effect on U.S. policy. Exile groups typically advocate very hardline policies. Tiananmen Square veterans in the United States lobbied the U.S. government vigorously to attach human rights conditions to China's most favored nation status in 1993 and to quash China's bid to host the Year 2000 Olympics.[12] But as they settle into their roles as professional exiles, these dissidents tend to have a sharply diminishing impact on political affairs in their own countries, particularly in states where regimes may bend but are not likely to break in the near future. Returnees from abroad may assume political roles when a civil war or other major conflict has been settled, as they did in Cambodia after the Paris peace agreement of 1991, but they are likely to have little effect in countries where political change is incremental and more peaceful.

Political émigrés from countries undergoing even modest reform tend to lose touch quickly with the political pulse of their societies. Over the past decade, the distance between Chinese exiled intellectuals in the West and their counterparts in China has widened noticeably on the question of political change. For example, in the debate this year on the United States' granting permanent normal trade relations (PTNR) to China, in-country Chinese liberals and dissidents advocated granting PNTR to Beijing, while some prominent exiled dissidents in the United States argued against it.[13] The great majority of in-country intellectuals who are reform-minded advocate individual rights and freedoms but recognize the inevitability of the state. Their plans for political reform are based on maintaining some degree of harmony with the state. Exiled dissidents, on the other hand, are more inclined to demand complete autonomy for civil society and to take a visibly hostile approach to the state.[14] This also reflects a process of natural selection. The most radical dissidents are likely to be the ones who are compelled to leave after a political confrontation or upheaval; once out, they have little incentive to modify their views. As social and political space gradually opens in authoritarian states, the exiled dissident's capital with his counterparts at home tends to diminish. There is less reason to see these figures as beacons of hope and more reason to focus on the in-country political process.

Although many activists believe that providing exiled dissidents with a base and a platform in the West strengthens their chances of influencing change in their home countries, doing so usually marginalizes them further. Since grant funds tend to go to the boldest and most outspoken, dissidents are subtly encouraged to reinforce Western ideas of political change in order to maintain their public profiles as well as their livelihood. These individuals may therefore appear out of touch and ineffectual to citizens in their home country. Their funding sources may also complicate their political image at home and tap into nationalist resentments. A large percentage of Chinese exile dissidents, for example, is funded by Taiwan.[15] The longer they remain abroad, the more difficult it may become for dissidents to organize with other nationals, even within the exile community. Most overseas communities have built-in political divisions. As time goes on and as competition for funds and the public spotlight becomes more intense, these splits tend to be exacerbated by personal rivalries and internecine squabbles.[16]

The Broadcast Model

The most deliberate attempt to follow cold war practice in the last decade has been the replication of the "surrogate" model of broadcast programming to the Soviet empire for several remaining authoritarian states. Since 1989, American politicians and democracy promoters have publicly tied the fall of communist regimes to the work of Radio Free Europe and Radio Liberty. Voice of America, the flagship international news service of the United States, also had a high profile in countries where freedom of expression was limited. The Radio Free Europe-Radio Liberty complex, however, reported "home" news: events and views it judged would be censored or opposed by the regime. It maintained that surrogate broadcasting provided a model of fair and objective reporting in an environment of total state control of the media. Radio Free Europe and Radio Liberty have been continued past the cold war as an aid to further democratization in Eastern Europe and the former Soviet Union. Dissident-statesmen such as Vaclav Havel in Czechoslovakia and Lech Walesa in Poland praised the American broadcast services when they took office after the cold war.[17]

In 1994 Congress authorized the establishment of Radio Free Asia, intended to broadcast in Burma, Cambodia, China (including Tibet), Laos, North Korea, and Vietnam. After several years of bureaucratic infighting, mostly over whether to launch a separate service or expand Voice of America's efforts in the region, Radio Free Asia broadcast its first programs in 1996.[18] Some initial attempts were made to soften the name of the Asia service; "Asia-Pacific Network" was suggested after noncommunist governments in the region criticized the program and Thailand refused to allow transmission from its territory.[19] Congress, however, was insistent on the "Radio Free" formula.

A year later, Congress authorized funds to establish Radio Free Iran, which began operation as an adjunct of Radio Free Europe.[20] Given the present state of relations with Saddam Hussein, Radio Free Iraq was inevitable. The United States also continues to operate Radio Marti for Cuba, a continuation of its service during the cold war, as well as a television version. TV Marti is the subject of continuing controversy in the United States, since it reportedly has not been able to penetrate a Cuban government block and does not actually reach viewers inside Cuba. Although legally independent, these services are fully funded by Congress.

Measuring the impact of such broad instruments is exceedingly difficult. As the first indicator of success, broadcast officials often point to the hostility these services evoke in the target regimes. Beyond predictable statements of condemnation, most of the governments are successful in jamming the surrogate broadcasts the majority of time, as they sometimes do with Voice of America.[21] This has given rise to a paradoxical standard of success in broadcast circles: the less access the general population has to the broadcast (because of the regime's demonstrated objection to it) the more successful it is. Regimes bristle not only at American claims that Radio Free Europe inspired the democratic resolutions in the former Soviet empire, but also at the memory of Radio Free Europe's involvement in encouraging the Hungarian Revolt in 1956. They refuse any suggestion that these present-day radio broadcasts differ from their cold war predecessors and regard them as instruments of propaganda.

Congress had anticipated this knee-jerk reaction, and enabling legislation for the surrogate services forbids the broadcasting of propaganda.[22] The officers in charge stress this fact in their public statements at regular intervals. This may be true in theory, if propaganda is defined as spreading exaggerations and falsehoods to support a doctrinal view, but the issue merits closer examination in practice. Rather than presenting a laboratory of free media, the content of these programs more often resembles a civics textbook on democratic principles. There is as well an element of shadow-boxing in the surrogate model. By attempting to counter regime censorship of specific information and curbs on individual writers it deems to be democratic, the service cannot apply objective criteria for its coverage. Instead, it essentially follows the regime's lead.

For example, regular features broadcast by Radio Free Asia in China include the life stories of Chinese dissidents, chronicles of the various democracy movements in China, and dissection of the elements of a democratic society.[23] The choice of commentators also raises questions about a balanced image. In recent years, Radio Free Asia has given the equivalent of a radio column to Tiananmen Square leader Wang Dan. But the most telling sign of a propagandistic approach, however subtle, is the language Radio Free Asia employs in describing its target countries. In 1998 congressional testimony one officer described farmer demonstrations ("peasant revolts") in Vietnam, which took place in a province he termed a "stronghold of communist militants,"[24] language that harks back to counterinsurgency programs of the 1960s and that oddly seems to bypass the broader communist takeover of Vietnam in 1975.

Outside the arena of mutual antagonism and charges of propagandizing, questions remain about the actual benefit of surrogate broadcasting on the development of media freedom in many of these countries. The Radio Free Europe model assumes a totalitarian society and a government choke-hold on all expression. This is undoubtedly the case in North Korea, but the position misrepresents the state of press freedom in a number of other target countries. An external actor that proports to hold the marker for free media in another society is making a bold claim. The deeper issue is whether such an ambition is a worthwhile goal in authoritarian states that are in the process of liberalizing. In these societies, attention (and assistance) are better focused on supporting the efforts of the society itself to expand expression and develop indigenous media capabilities.

The Helsinki Model

By far the most ambitious attempts to graft a cold war mechanism onto present-day policy toward authoritarian countries are various proposals from Western countries to replicate the Helsinki process. In generic terms, this refers to a regional framework that monitors the observation of human rights in each member state and so pressures governments to improve protection. The cold war prototype for this framework was the Conference on Security and Cooperation in Europe (CSCE), which arose from the Helsinki Final Act of 1975. Drawing in the countries of Eastern and Western Europe, the Soviet Union, the United States, and Canada, the CSCE administered a comprehensive regime of cooperative efforts divided among three "baskets": security, economic relations, and humanitarian issues. Within the third basket was a general agreement to encourage the protection of civil, political, economic, social, and cultural rights. After the cold war, the CSCE became the Organization for Security and Cooperation in Europe and has taken an active role in promoting human rights and democracy in Eastern Europe.

The CSCE was a loose arrangement that scarcely threatened the prior division of its member states into two separate political, military, and economic blocs. On the contrary, in some ways it reinforced those blocs. The Soviets acceded to the Helsinki Act (in fact, urged it upon Washington) because it implicitly recognized the post–World War II territorial and ideological division of Europe and provided the Eastern bloc with greater access to Western markets and technology.[25] At the time, Moscow considered the price of these gains—that is, the human rights provisions of Basket Three—to be negligible.

However, human rights reporting requirements were imposed upon CSCE members. These provisions strengthened the development of a small but activist civil society in some Eastern bloc nations. In-country Helsinki committees gave dissidents an organizational structure, as well as an ostensible reason for monitoring their governments' human rights performance, although they also made it easier for regimes to root out and punish dissidents. The results were uneven but the success stories were compelling. The Czech Helsinki Committee formed the nucleus of dissident activity and provided much of the leadership for the "velvet revolution" of 1989. In Bulgaria and Romania, however, repression was so effective that monitoring groups were never formed. Members of the Moscow Helsinki group were regularly harassed and arrested, even after Mikhail Gorbachev's reforms had begun.[26] Nevertheless, the Helsinki process provided the scaffolding that enabled a rudimentary, if extremely restricted, civil society to grow in some communist states. It also offered a regular and more disciplined channel for Western governments to criticize the human rights record of Eastern bloc regimes.

During the 1990s some Western governments saw in the Helsinki process a tool to press authoritarian regimes to protect human rights and encourage greater political freedoms that was in keeping with the new post–cold war spirit of multilateralism. However, few regions have the degree of formal integration that characterized cold war Europe on both sides of the political divide. The regions that hold many of the authoritarian states of concern to the United States are poor candidates for regional engineering from the outside. Nevertheless, policymakers have attempted to apply the Helsinki model to Asia because of the region's perceived symmetry with cold war communism. China and other Leninists states, they assume, could become enmeshed in the network of human rights reports and groups that bound the Soviet bloc governments but loosened their civil societies. Such an arrangement might also counteract the "Asian values" view of Western governments bludgeoning Asian societies with complaints and conditionality by inviting Western and Asian nations to critique one another's human rights performance.

In 1990 Australian foreign minister Gareth Evans proposed the creation of a Commission for Security and Cooperation in Asia (CSCA) that would mirror the CSCE. His initial plan was for a security arrangement alone; in time, he reasoned, a human rights "basket" could be added to the framework.[27] Australia's failure to make headway on this proposal was due not to explicit resistance on human rights—discussion with Asian governments had not reached that point—but to a more fundamental cause. Unlike Africa, which is currently considering a proposal to build a Helsinki-type process on the longstanding structure of the Organization for African Unity, Asia has no strong panregional underpinnings.[28] Significant differences in political systems and mutual suspicions (particularly in Northeast Asia) make it difficult to organize the entire region along any one line. Australia has since abandoned its comprehensive CSCE-like proposal and has focused on establishing a network of Asian national human rights commissions, the

Asia-Pacific Forum of National Human Rights Institutions. Not surprisingly, only the democratic nations of Asia have joined, although Burma is reportedly considering forming a commission.[29] At the present time, it is doubtful that prefabricated regional intergovernmental organizations (particularly those imported from the West) that address domestic political practices will be able to recruit Asia's authoritarian states.

Regardless, in recent years several initiatives have been proposed in the U.S. Congress to press a CSCE framework upon Asia, this time skipping over a security regime and focusing immediately on human rights. They are intended to help break the logjam of engagement-versus-confrontation in the U.S. policy debate on human rights in China, by moving the issue to a multilateral track.[30] Although this might help solve an American domestic political problem, Asians see little benefit in such proposals. Asian governments are reluctant to join initiatives formulated with the transparent purpose of censuring an individual nation in the region, particularly if doing so would disturb new relations with former adversaries. They are doubly wary of efforts to target China, a point they made repeatedly through the 1990s when the West tried to rally the region behind a resolution criticizing Beijing at the United Nations Human Rights Commission.[31]

The U.S. proposals also lack the bait-and-switch incentives of the original CSCE, although it is doubtful that even those would work in the Asian case. Moscow's acceptance of a human rights basket in exchange for cooperation on security and trade was a blunder of historic proportions. Hypersensitive to the lessons of the Soviet Union's collapse, Beijing is unlikely to make such a miscalculation.

The irony of these false starts is that the impetus to develop frameworks to encourage civil and political freedoms in these "hold-out" regions is more likely to come from their own emerging civil societies. The Helsinki model assumes that external forces (intergovernmental ones at that) are needed to jump-start civil groups and to build regional arrangements for the protection of rights. In Asia and the Middle East, the reverse is likely to be true, although development of such frameworks will be a long-term process.

Informal networks of human rights nongovernmental organizations are criss-crossing the Asia region. Although there are some panregional NGO networks, groupings are particularly strong in Southeast Asia, where thirty years of formal organization under the Association of Southeast Asian Nations (ASEAN) has stimulated parallel NGO efforts. In return, Southeast Asian

NGOs are pressing their governments for intergovernmental human rights regimes. Southeast Asia is also experimenting with new arrangements that cross old lines of political division. Both nongovernmental networks and ASEAN are launching cooperative projects that encompass the Mekong River region, in subject areas ranging from human resource development to law. As a Mekong country, China is also eligible to participate, as are Vietnam and Laos.

In the Middle East, NGO initiatives substitute for a functional inter-governmental organization on human rights. The Arab Organization for Human Rights issues annual reports on human rights conditions in the countries of the Arab world, and a number of subregional NGO networks are being established.[32]

This phenomenon of indigenous, informal regional groupings forming to support human rights calls into question the need for officially framed, Western-driven arrangements at this time. In regions where some of the key powers are authoritarian states with entrenched regimes, the latter model will not work, structurally or strategically. In these cases, the potential for Western leadership lies not in proposing off-the-shelf institutions but in quietly supporting these emerging trends.

Pressure and Punishment

For all of the reasons that make the authoritarian countries in this study draw heat in the U.S. policy community—repressive practices toward their citizens, concerns about their reliability as international partners, historic tensions—the policy instruments of first resort tend to be criticism and conditionality. In American foreign policy, ideological foes are publicly confronted. The press conference debates on human rights in the 1997–98 U.S.-China sum-mits were the direct descendants of Vice President Richard Nixon's "kitchen debates" in Moscow with Soviet president Nikita Krushchev. Because of their showmanship, these exercises have some value in maintaining domestic interest in foreign policy. They frequently have short-term impact on rela-tions with an authoritarian country. However, there is significantly less evi-dence that they are effective in influencing the long-term process of political change in these countries.

In policy debates over authoritarian regimes, form and content are often confused. The battle lines on human rights policy for China, which were drawn annually in the 1990s over renewal of most favored nation status, typically weigh the use of sanctions (or their threat) against more modulated forms of criticism that can be accommodated within a policy of engagement. In more than a decade of debate on this issue, the question has seldom been raised whether the conditions set out with these instruments would, if they were met, contribute to genuine political change.

For a policy of pressure to be seen as successful in the U.S. domestic population it must deliver concrete results in short order. These indicators of success are chosen unilaterally. Under the circumstances, genuine dialogue or negotiation between the two countries on a coherent set of steps is not possible. Nor is the political will needed in the regime to support greater openness likely to increase in such a state of siege. As a result, the demander often resorts to conditions which have symbolic value but negligible effect on long-term political development. Even so, the target nation seldom complies.

For example, the requirements in President William Clinton's 1993 executive order that conditioned the renewal of China's most favored nation status on human rights improvements were heavily focused on political prisoners.[33] Accounting for imprisoned dissidents, refraining from using them in prison labor, allowing the International Committee of the Red Cross to check on their condition, and releasing prominent prisoners on medical parole were key elements of the order.[34] These were admirable humanitarian objectives, but it is difficult to see how even the short-term political environment would have been affected if the Chinese government had consented to these demands.

Beijing may well reason that it is better to keep the controversy (and the conditionality) focused on measures that have no lasting effect than to drift into areas that present a more meaningful threat to the regime. Accordingly, it keeps this dynamic going by releasing high-profile dissidents on an individual basis, strategically timed. In a single motion, the prisoner exchanges the prison for the jetliner and is flown out of the country, often to the United States. The United States declares victory, pressure is relieved on Beijing for the time being, and the dissident has been removed from the Chinese political environment.

Westerners often protest China's use of political prisoners in this way,[35] but they tend to ignore the larger truth that dissident poker is a game that takes two to play. It too is a cold war routine, first devised between Moscow and Washington. Some analysts point out, however, that it can have the perverse effect of prolonging a dissident's time in jail, by linking his release to other aspects of the relationship. Beijing appeared ready to release Wang Dan in 1997, but delayed because of the "donor-gate" scandal.[36] It may also have unintended consequences with the broader society in an authoritarian country by suggesting that the United States cares only about the fate of a chosen few individuals.[37]

A second problem with an all-pressure policy is that it often escalates from criticism, which can have a constructive effect on foreign relations, to condemnation and, in time, to ritual condemnation. Such exercises tend to take on a life of their own and follow a cyclical pattern apart from current conditions or specific events in the target country. Resolutions condemning a country's human rights record before the United Nations Human Rights Commission are entered at the annual spring meeting in Geneva and take months of planning. Congressional actions, ranging from resolutions to more punitive measures, are more flexible but must follow the legislative process. The predictability of some of these exercises diminishes their effect and convinces the target government that they are directed not so much at the regime as at domestic audiences.

Most authoritarian countries are subject to a variety of sanctions or the threat of sanctions. Some are the object of categorical restrictions in U.S. legislation, such as the prohibition of aid to communist countries in the Foreign Assistance Act. Nations normalizing relations or seeking trade preferences from the United States are held to a number of conditions, some of which bear upon civil and political rights. There are also numerous country-specific prohibitions, such as those imposed on China after the Tiananmen Square crackdown.

Sanctions may address a range of policy areas from human rights to nuclear proliferation. Studies suggest, however, that they have little effect on the long-term domestic political behavior of regimes or the development of institutions of social and political pluralism.[38] As with other instruments of pressure in this policy area, it is difficult to set objectives for sanctions policy that are both attainable and effective. Sticks wielded from the outside seldom generate the subtle attitudinal shifts and internal maneuvers typical of the early stages of liberalization, a time when the main drive is internal pressure. And as with dissident poker, sanctions can at times be counterproductive. They may strengthen the regime's internal popularity by creating a siege mentality or by stirring nationalist resentments. Broad-based economic sanctions that create internal scarcity may also fortify the regime by giving it greater control over the distribution of goods.[39]

A final problem with policy dominated by conditionality is that it is often difficult to follow through with the dire consequences threatened. This is particularly true when intangibles, such as the political systems of other countries, are at issue, rather than transnational threats (for example, arms proliferation or terrorism) that may directly threaten the security of American citizens. Trade is a central component of policies among some authoritarian nations, and the American public itself may stand to suffer from some sanctions, if only mildly. Domestic debate on trade-offs in sanctions policy toward these countries can result in long-term stalemate.

These countervailing interests are amplified at the multilateral level, when attempts are made to persuade other countries to join in serious threats or forms of punishment to influence a third country's internal political processes. In the post–cold war period, considerable progress has been made in organizing the established democracies to support the consolidation of new democratic brethren. Democracy assistance programs are coordinated among donors, and joint demarches are common among Western diplomats in countries where democracy (or the observance of the human rights expected of a democracy) is in danger. Regions that are predominantly democratic, such as Latin America, are now willing to introduce democratic norms into regional organizations. Through these regional mechanisms, member states may unite to prevent democratic backsliding in a neighboring state or to punish the overthrow of a democratic government. In the post–cold war period, when countries pledge themselves formally to democracy, the international community is more inclined than ever to hold them to their word.

In the face of persistent authoritarianism, however, the cohesiveness of the democracy club breaks down. Fault lines frequently emerge around trade issues, but there are also deeper differences on the best way to handle recalcitrant regimes. The annual Western tradition of attempting to pass a resolution against China in the United Nations Human Rights Commission foundered in 1997 when the European Union declined to play its usual role of introducing the resolution or to support it at all. Americans were quick to charge that Europeans were speaking from their pocketbooks, but by that time there was evidence of genuine disagreement over the path of political change in China. Europeans had demonstrated a preference for strengthening ties with in-country moderates over the American fashion of supporting exiled dissidents on the farthest end of the liberal spectrum. By the late 1990s, assistance funds were helping to strengthen the village election system in China,[40] while the U.S. Congress continued to reject proposals from the administration to apply modest funds to similar programs in China. A clearer division is evident when Japan is petitioned to join in putative measures to encourage change in authoritarian states, particularly in the Asia region. In contrast to the Western democracies, it is not self-evident to Japan that its democratic system carries a missionary clause.[41]

The discussion in this chapter is focused on cold war assumptions and instruments in present U.S. policy toward authoritarian countries. This lingering paradigm does not represent the full range of American opinion, and it is not applied uniformly for every state that fails to live up to democratic expectations. However, the paradigm still holds the deciding vote in many debates on policy to influence political change in key authoritarian states. Despite its resonance with many Americans, there is little evidence in the post–cold war period that this framework is effective, particularly in liberalizing societies. To construct a policy that is more nuanced in the present requires a more nuanced view of the past.

5

Supporting Liberalization without Sinking It: Recommendations and Conclusions

The United States needs to reorient its approach and revise its policies to promote political change in authoritarian countries that show signs of opening their systems. Unless and until it does so, U.S. policy toward these countries will be antagonizing and ineffective for the most part and will, ironically, harm the chances that liberal gains in these countries can be sustained.

These policy changes are not likely to damage U.S. relations with countries of strategic or economic importance or with the reformers within these countries; on the contrary, they are likely to improve them. A new policy will not be significantly more expensive, in part because it will permit some funds (such as those for international broadcast radio) to be reprogrammed. By comparison, assistance grants in the liberalization process are usually smaller and more circumspect than many democracy promotion projects initiated after the cold war. There is, however, the question of scale. A modest assistance program for a liberalizing China may require a larger budget than the present "radicals and radios" approach and may even exceed full-strength democratization programs in smaller countries. Presumably, a more effective strategy for promoting peaceful change in the world's largest country would justify the higher cost.

No significant structural changes are required in the American foreign policy apparatus. Instead, the most important change is the most difficult one—forging a new policy paradigm. For such a policy to work at all in many of these authoritarian systems, foreign governments and assistance donors must curb their expectations for an immediate democratic outcome. Political liberalization must be seen and supported as an end in itself. This calls for a suspension of the democratic imperative and of many elements of a democracy promotion framework, however temporarily.

Some aspects of the liberalization process make Americans uncomfortable, particularly those who subscribe to strict ideological views. The dual-purpose nature of liberalization, which may benefit and even strengthen the regime in the short term, may be perceived as counterintuitive and might even make policy efforts appear counterproductive at times. The invisible line that prohibits (and may punish) movement toward an organized political opposition can be difficult to acknowledge, even on a temporary basis. It is not necessary nor is it desirable for Americans to embrace these limits, but it is important to be cognizant of them.

Although it can be an uncertain process, liberalization does have a template and a sequence of a gradual widening of the regime spectrum and a gradual strengthening of civil society. These processes can vary more widely from one country to the next than in the democratization process, which is itself often sui generis. Policy responses therefore require greater flexibility. Nevertheless, a number of common tactical guidelines should be considered. Some of these apply to interaction with the liberalizing regime and society, others reconfigure relations within the U.S. policy community, and others aim to expand the policy toolbox.

1. Keep slightly behind the curve.

Democracy promotion after the cold war is often structured as a tutorial relationship between the established democracy donor and the consolidating democracy recipient. The donor's role in this relationship is to stay ahead of democratic progress in the recipient country. Assistance officials may help develop road maps for institutional reform, advise political parties on campaigns, or volunteer their recommendations on the development of nongovernmental organizations. They typically take a problem-solving approach, rooting out the weaknesses in the system. Donors often see themselves, and may be seen in the host country, as partners in political change. In the late 1980s and early 1990s, with political systems turning over on a daily basis, freelance Western experts circled the globe, helping rewrite constitutions, redesign legal systems, and cobble together host-country nongovernmental organizations.

Foreign donors and other actors who support political liberalization in authoritarian countries cannot and should not assume such architectural roles. In contrast to the more open climate in democratizing societies, in authoritarian systems nearly all formal agenda-setting is done by the host country, usually by the government. Outside opinions and suggestions may be solicited or offered informally and are often accepted. However, the basic modus operandi should be to respond to host country requests and initiatives. Those external actors who place themselves ahead of the system's capacity or capability often see their projects collapse under their own weight. Those who get out in front of political will almost always suffer a government, or even nationalist, backlash.

Foreign assistance donors and government officials should therefore articulate an unexceptional set of objectives and attempt to link them with broad, established national goals. A back-and-fill approach is often the most productive one. For example, it is often better to focus on the implementation of legal protections already written into law than to propose new areas for legal reform.

Similarly, external actors should exercise caution in making claims about the results of their assistance and in advertising that aid. Democracy promoters are often prone to exaggerating the connections between their efforts and the adoption of specific reforms or even the nation's overall political progress. They face stiff competition from other democracy groups and pressure from their own funders to demonstrate that their activities have impact. In authoritarian countries that are beginning to open, ownership of the liberalization process should not be challenged in this way.

2. Take a disciplined approach to rhetoric.

Chest-pounding and finger-wagging are common techniques in U.S. foreign relations, particularly with authoritarian governments. These measures may damage relations with the target country but they rarely destroy them—authoritarian regimes are themselves masters of rhetorical rage. But in authoritarian states that are liberalizing, or whose regimes are seriously considering such a step, an undisciplined, high-decibel approach in urging political change can do more than disturb short-term equanimity between the two countries. It can forfeit the opportunity for genuine impact, however small.

A more constructive approach to rhetoric in these circumstances was illustrated by the farewell speech of U.S. ambassador Paul Wolfowitz in

Indonesia in 1989. Wolfowitz was ending a successful three-year tour, having earned a reputation as a diplomat who had developed a wide array of Indonesian contacts and an in-depth knowledge of the country. At that point in Suharto's rule, the first signs of openness (*keterbukaan*) were appearing. A former head of the internal security agency, General Sumitro, had just published a critical article in an international journal urging that Indonesia adopt a more representative parliamentary system and a presidential contest with more than one candidate. Using that entry point, Wolfowitz called for greater political pluralism in his remarks, being careful to use the term *keterbukaan* and to avoid the word *democracy*.[1]

The Wolfowitz speech drew widespread attention within the country and was echoed with calls for liberalization and wider public debate from several Indonesian quarters. This internal pressure reinforced Suharto's inclination at the time to begin experimenting with greater openness. Indonesian scholars credit Wolfowitz with giving a timely boost to the start of a five-year period of relaxation. Although forward-leaning, the ambassador's actions were acceptable to a wide range of Indonesians. The speech supported the recommendations of an insider, rather than a marginal figure or an anti-regime dissident. Other key factors were Wolfowitz's bona fides with Indonesian society, his timing in building on Sumitro's opening volley rather than taking the first step himself, and his careful choice of language.

3. Give the perspectives of country specialists greater weight in policy decisions to promote political change and the edge in judgment calls.

In the post–cold war climate of global democratization and stronger human rights regimes, specialists on authoritarian countries often do not fare well in debates on policy to encourage political development. They are frequently seen as being too cautious, even collaborationist, in their approach. (In the polarized climate of the debates on most favored nation trading status for China, for example, American China specialists were sometimes referred to by human rights activists as *sinapologists*.) Some country specialists, particularly those from cold war generations, are in fact hostile to the idea of encouraging internal change in these countries and prefer to limit policy to security concerns and trade issues. However, the younger generation of specialists tends to have more extensive awareness of domestic political issues and greater interest in promoting political change in an appropriate manner.

Universalists, on the other hand, tend to focus their vision on sweeping trends and global standards and so may miss the modest openings that typify the liberalization process in authoritarian countries. Country specialists are better able to place these small gains in context, without overselling them or dismissing them altogether. They are often skilled at interpreting coded messages issued by authoritarian regimes that may indicate a new political trend, in either direction. They are also able to assess the actual damage from major setbacks. During the late 1990s, American television viewers were still reminded of the 1989 crackdown in Tiananmen Square because news reports on China almost invariably open with famous footage of a lone protester, clutching only a shopping bag, blocking the path of a tank. By the early 1990s, however, many of the restrictions imposed upon citizens immediately after the crackdown had been quietly rescinded. Although China-watchers were well aware of this, the American popular media did not catch up until President Clinton's 1998 trip to China sparked a round of reports on conditions inside the country.

Country specialists are also less likely to be thrown by the contradictory nature of liberalization in these countries when, as China specialist Harry Harding noted, "there will be good news and bad news simultaneously."[2] They may therefore be more constitutionally suited to a long-term process. When universalists are off to more promising situations or more dramatic crises, the country specialist continues to mark the smaller gains and losses of incremental change. The solution is not to shun universalists, who can bring a comparative perspective to the policy debate, but to break this polarization with a more integrated mix.

4. Avoid the temptation to personalize the process.
Westerners often look for familiar reference points when they attempt to interpret other political cultures. They may canonize figures they perceive to be progressive and demonize those they believe to be hard-line. There are compelling reasons to curb this practice during liberalization.

First, accurate and complete information on the negotiations and internal deliberations of authoritarian regimes is seldom available to outsiders. External actors who rely on fragments are likely to miscalculate the internal political dynamics of the regime and the position of regime members in the power structure that underlies the formal system. Second, championing individuals within the liberalization process can tie foreign officials and assistance groups to figures who may be in one week and out the next; it may be some time before they realize that "their" moderate has fallen out of favor. Moreover, attempts to influence the politics of liberalization from the outside by anointing some individuals as more democratic than others may backfire, on the individual and his sponsors. It is important during the liberalization period for outsiders to resist viewing the regime as a monolith, but it is equally important to maintain a nonpartisan flexibility with regime members whenever possible.

Depending on the level of support, an overly partisan approach may also reinforce the personal nature of politics in authoritarian systems and make it more difficult for power to be redistributed or for institutions to become more pluralistic. This can be the case even in new democracies, where executive power continues to eclipse that of the other branches and where political parties frequently coalesce around individuals. U.S. policy toward Russia for most of the 1990s and into the present decade has been a function of support for individual leaders, because Russian national policy remains rooted in personalities rather than in broadly conceived platforms. Without doubt, establishing and maintaining positive relations with Russia's head of state is vital to U.S. interests. However, a personalized approach to democracy promotion—as opposed to broader support for institution-building and the development of civil society—has ironically helped to reinforce the paradigm of strongman government still rooted in Russian political culture.

5. Don't mistake a diplomatic opening for an internal political one.
Normalizing relations with a former enemy often encourages a romantic illusion in which the desire to forge new friendships causes each side to believe that the other is becoming more like itself. Thus Americans often assume that closer ties with an authoritarian state are an indication that it is democratizing, because democracy and the protection of rights are part of our national self-image. Moreover, officials from the other country who are assigned the task of negotiating closer relations are often Western-leaning moderates whom the government has chosen as special handlers. Westerners may assume that they typify the regime as a whole and underestimate the strength of hard-liners. They may also assume that increased contact with the West will create greater political openness in the other society by reflex.

Although this may have been the case on some occasions (the Democracy Wall movement in China corresponded to the normalization of U.S.-China relations in the late 1970s), these initial surges are usually easy for the regime to control. Authoritarian governments are well equipped to separate foreign affairs from domestic ones. Normalization and increased contact no doubt give the West greater opportunity to influence both reformers and conservatives in an authoritarian state, but they cannot effect change in the absence of domestic political will. For example, as U.S. official and private relations with North Korea expand, Americans should not expect to see an immediate shift toward greater political pluralism.

Conversely, a society in the midst of political and social liberalization should not automatically be assumed to be becoming more pro-Western or pro-American. U.S.-Iranian relations have not improved at the same pace that Iranian political processes are liberalizing. On the contrary, Iranian reformers have some reason to exercise restraint in reconfiguring relations with the United States in order to maintain internal equilibrium with powerful conservative elements. Moreover, an informal reading of domestic opinion in Iran suggests that reformers' attitudes on nuclear weapons and some terrorist groups do not line up exactly with American views.[3]

6. Give human rights a supporting, rather than leading, role in liberalization policy.

In U.S. policies toward authoritarian countries, human rights concerns often represent the sum total of efforts to promote political openness. However, human rights frameworks do not easily convert into road maps for political change. Although rights groups do not explicitly take positions on the best system of government for specific countries, they demand a level of human rights protection that is rarely found outside an established liberal democracy. Liberalizing states seldom achieve this level, although improving rights is a reasonable goal for liberalization. In human rights policy, all rights are accorded equal weight, and the notion of a sequence in developing the protection of rights is strongly resisted. By contrast, liberalization is an incomplete process that is allowed to go forward *because* it is sequenced.

In addition, human rights policy tends to focus on the plight of the most oppressed individuals and of fringe populations. Liberalization, on the other hand, tends to expand the rights of the elite strata first and then of the majority population. The rights of dissidents and minorities are usually not taken into consideration in this period. Human rights groups are under-standably uncomfortable with this order. When the U.S. Department of State made minor alterations to methodology in its 1997 human rights report on China, citing positive changes in administrative law and the expansion of personal freedoms outside the political realm, it created a furor in the human rights community. Activists charged that the U.S. government had capitulated to Beijing by mentioning improvements in the "lives of everyday citizens" when two thousand political prisoners remained in detention.

Yet during periods of authoritarian rule, even relaxed ones, the majority group is seldom concerned with the rights of the periphery. In Indonesia, for example, the suppression of separatists in Aceh, Irian Jaya, and East Timor went unchallenged by the general population for decades. It was when the country was thrust precipitously into a democratization process that public awareness of the rights of these groups began to emerge.[4] U.S. policy should not neglect the oppressed and disadvantaged, but their place in the political structure and the society should be assessed more realistically. Policies to pro-mote liberalization that are driven primarily by human rights concerns may be out of synch with the aspirations of the majority in an authoritarian soci-ety and gain little domestic support in that country as a result.

Lastly, the process of liberalization, with its ambiguities and half-steps, tends to make human rights groups uneasy. They are reluctant to reward the level of human rights protection that liberalization typically achieves and fear that doing so will impede further progress. They worry in particular that West-ern governments will soften their demands for human rights protection in lib-eralizing states. They are often inclined therefore to insist that gains during the liberalization period are not genuine.[5] U.S. policy should not abandon con-cern for human rights, but it should take into account that the long-term guar-antee of rights is a more open political system and a more vigilant society.

7. Don't insist on perfect checks and balances or a strict separation between state and society.

Policymakers sometimes place more stringent requirements upon the insti-tutions in an authoritarian system than on those in democratizing societies, where institutional amphibiousness may also linger.[6] During the liberalization period, external actors should expect to encounter (and to work with) state institutions under the influence of the regime and civil society organizations with links to the government. Rather than focusing on institutions, they should make processes their greater concern. The objective should be to advance pluralism within the formal system, which may lead to greater accountability, and to support the growth and competence of civil society organizations. The shape of the institution is not the point at this stage. Rather, it is the direction in which it is moving and the momentum for change.

This could translate into helping nongovernmental organizations break new ground in autonomy, even though they remain under some governmental controls. It may also lead to aid for government ministries charged with implementing liberal reforms.[7] The latter also enables outside actors to support moderates and reformers within government without intruding into the political process in an overtly partisan manner.

8. During the early stages of liberalization, think "social" rather than "political."

When an authoritarian government and society take an instrumental approach to political change in the early stages of liberalization, outside actors would do well to follow suit. As with the role of institutional change during liberalization, the focus is not so much on specific sectors but on wherever new freedoms are emerging. This could mean supporting governments in their attempts to introduce or strengthen rule of law for economic reasons or assisting nongovernmental organizations in disaster relief efforts in countries where that had been an exclusive government function. In addition to being the more effective route, an instrumental approach is likely to be a safer one. During this period, a foreign official or donor who proceeds directly to a political agenda will quickly be seen as anti-regime and may even be viewed by ordinary citizens with suspicion.

9. Keep benchmarks in mind, but don't demand instant results.

A policy that aims to promote political liberalization, as distinct from democratization, requires a separate set of criteria for evaluation. Without benchmarks that take the nature of liberalization into account, policymakers will be compelled to rely exclusively upon indicators for democratic development or on a narrow human rights framework.

Whenever possible, indicators of progress in liberalization should hone to specific country situations and be developed with input from host country interlocutors. These measurements are less quantifiable than the criteria for democratic development because they seek to capture attitudinal changes and trends that are nascent at best. The views of host country analysts are doubly important in evaluation because outside evaluators may be restricted by the government in their efforts to determine the full impact of initiatives.

In comparison to democratization, liberalization often takes a more circuitous path and requires a different timeline. Benchmarks must therefore build in more patience and flexibility. After the fall of the Berlin Wall, Senator Richard Lugar warned that "The world [has] . . . an attention span too short for the development and growth of democracy."[8] This admonition applies doubly to the liberalization process. By charting the course of liberalization, benchmarks may also help to explain it and hold the attention of policymakers and funders for a longer time.

Some will consider it unpalatable, even un-American, to parse repression and designate some levels of authoritarian rule to be more acceptable than others. However, development of realistic indicators will help determine which signs of openness are becoming less arbitrary and are therefore more likely to endure.

10. Work through regional networks and institutions but let regional norms take the lead.

Regional networks can be useful for encouraging openness in authoritarian states in the long term. In the past, the United States has attempted to use these organizations as surrogates. Efforts to persuade them to impose sanctions upon a member state for human rights abuses or to exclude an authoritarian government from membership have seldom been successful. In regions where authoritarian and democratic states are mixed, regional institutions tend to follow rules of noninterference in the domestic affairs of member states. This may change as the democratic balance begins to shift in some regions. For example, in recent years the Association of Southeast Asian Nations (ASEAN) has debated proposals from their democratic members to move from the traditional ASEAN principle of noninterference to one of "flexible engagement," which would allow the group to take positions when a member's internal affairs affect other states or the region as a whole. Such proposals have yet to win consensus, but a democratizing Indonesia could tilt the balance toward a more interventionist approach. Lacking democratic solidarity, however, in ASEAN as in other regions, institutions will usually heed the least common denominator.

The role of the United States in some regional institutions is indirect at best. During the cold war, the United States was a member of the Conference on Security and Cooperation in Europe and remains a driving force in the OSCE. The United States has been the most influential member of the Organization of American States since its inception. But in other regions, the U.S. is a "dialogue partner" at most and is not in a position to inject concern for domestic political affairs into the framework. Attempts to start new regional organizations for this purpose, as seen in the Helsinki model, are not likely to succeed.

To make more effective use of regional organizations that include authoritarian states, the United States should approach them with broad goals and eschew specific political outcomes for the time being. Supporting nongovernmental networks that take up issues of political and social freedom may be one of the most immediate and effective routes, but it is important to let these groups develop along their own lines. Intergovernmental organizations also merit attention, although they are usually less forward-leaning than NGO groups. One near-term objective should be to encourage these organizations to place long-term political development issues, such as broad legal norms, on their agendas. Another should be to integrate authoritarian states into the regional framework to the fullest extent possible (in inter-parliamentary groups or regional lawyers associations, for example), even though the participating bodies from authoritarian states are likely to be closer to the regime than those from democratic states.

The power of the demonstration effect can be overstated, but exposure to other political systems (and to the economic and social benefits of these systems) can have subliminal influence on the leaders and citizens of authoritarian societies, particularly if they have been isolated from their neighbors in recent history. Using regional organizations in policies toward authoritarian countries should be seen as investments in long-term political development. In the short term, however, regimes are likely to ensure that their own experiments in openness stop at the water's edge.

11. Reserve sanctions (if any) for obvious reversals of established democratic processes.
The reasons for this are self-evident, but they are worth summarizing. The liberalization process is not conducive to conditionality, because it is a matter of shifting relationships rather than formal institutional change. Sanctions

cannot easily penetrate or influence the dynamic of relations within a regime, where political pluralism often begins and where decisions about further openness are made. This rules out the use of even targeted or "smart" sanctions. Although they are more specific than broad-based economic sanctions, they cannot be sufficiently tuned to discriminate between regime progressives and hard-liners. What gains might be achieved through sanctions during the liberalization period, such as the release of dissidents, are likely to be inconsequential.

Domestic support for sanctions can be difficult to secure, particularly when economic interests are at stake. Support for multilateral sanctions can be even more problematic, since potential sanctions partners may differ on models of political change as well as be restricted by their own national interests. Lastly, attempts to apply conditionality through regional organizations are not likely to succeed in regions where authoritarian governments have significant sway.

12. Let nongovernmental organizations (NGOs) take the lead in providing assistance.

"Official" U.S. policy to encourage change in authoritarian societies is often steeped in cold war models and the post–cold war democracy framework. Paradigm shifts in foreign policy are not accomplished through sudden epiphanies but by successive layers of change. However, immediate strategies to support liberalization can be implemented by working through American NGOs.

Arguably, NGOs are the better agents to promote liberalization even when official policy is in tune with that process. They have built-in distance (and deniability) from the U.S. government and may therefore be less threatening to regimes. As a result, they are often able to work with a wide range of government officials and local NGO staff on issues that would be too sensitive for official attention. They are less subject to the trade-offs that can distort implementation of official policy and thus are better able to pursue long-term objectives. Their relative autonomy from their own government, in comparison to host country civil society organizations, can serve as an implicit NGO model. Finally, NGOs are able to maintain a lower profile than official agencies, which are compelled to publicize their efforts. The brass plaque syndrome—which dictates that every sack of grain and every facility built with government funds should carry some advertisement of the donor—can capsize sensitive efforts to support liberalization.

The greatest strength of NGOs—their nonofficial status—is occasionally their greatest weakness as well. However contentious official bilateral relations may be, most governments are reluctant to break them off completely once they have been established. Authoritarian regimes have far less hesitation and suffer little consequence in ordering a foreign NGO that has caused offense out of the country or in otherwise preventing one from operating there.

But this too can be an indicator of the strength or weakness of the liberalization process. On the whole, authoritarian governments view the presence of foreign NGOs to be in their interest, for diplomatic as well as development reasons. One of the earliest signs of an opening in rigid authoritarian systems is often permission for foreign NGOs to operate, usually under very restrictive circumstances. This may occur in advance of diplomatic normalization with the country, making the NGO a stalking horse for both governments.

13. Use multipurpose organizations rather than "democracy gangs" and field-based groups rather than "parachute" operations.

Conventional wisdom in the official policy community holds that specialized democracy promotion agencies and NGOs are best suited to encourage political change in authoritarian countries. In this view, their strength lies in their ability to identify democratizing trends, to work with opposition groups, and to help countries manage transitions to democracy. But these factors argue against using them during the early stages of the liberalization process. The imposition of a democracy framework restricts the group to a narrow political dimension and to individuals who are willing to identify themselves as reformers or prodemocracy activists. Their exclusive democracy focus may prejudice regimes against them and restrict access to government channels. In evaluations of their activities, they are likely to characterize liberalization only by the degree to which it resembles, or departs from, democratization.

The optimum external organization to promote liberalization is a multipurpose one, with experience in political development as one of several program areas. These groups are usually able to work in authoritarian countries earlier than democracy organizations because they can offer assistance in less sensitive areas. Their program range gives them the contacts and the bona fides to work with a wider spectrum of actors, as befits the instrumental character of many liberalization experiments. Through crosscutting activities, these organizations can support convergence in the liberalization process, nurturing ties between legislators and NGOs or between journalists and advocacy groups. They are better designed for longevity. In times of backsliding, multipurpose organizations can maintain their involvement in the country through program activities that stay well away from the political process. Finally, if liberalization does proceed to democratization, these organizations are better positioned to support that transition than most democracy organizations, which tend to awaken to events in the country at the time of a democratic transition. The "parachute" approach of many democracy organizations can be wasteful and costly as newly arrived assistance officials scramble for contacts and program activities in the lead-up to a transitional election or other democratic watershed.

Conventional wisdom also holds that "offshore" organizations are preferable to those that maintain a resident operation in authoritarian countries. Because they are less susceptible to control or reprisal by the regime, they are viewed as having more freedom of movement. Although this is technically true, it does not compensate for the inherent weaknesses of such a structure. Without a continuous presence, assistance officials have difficulty developing nuanced views of the political situation or a wide base of contacts. They are at risk of funding groups that can articulate the goals of Western organizations but may in reality have little impact. By contrast, field-based organizations are able to identify and support indigenous groups and individuals who may be less polished but are more influential.

An example of the ability of a field-based, multipurpose organization to support liberalization can be found in the program of the Asia Foundation, an American quasi-nongovernmental organization, in Taiwan from 1977 to 1987. With several years of prior experience in Taiwan, the Foundation was able to detect and support the first openings in the late 1970s, through projects such as legal assistance to strengthen the "demand" side of the rule of law. In the early 1980s, the Foundation provided support to Taiwanese NGOs that gradually became more activist in a number of issue areas, including the environment, consumer rights, and women's rights. It also supported artistic groups and editorial cartoonists who were pushing the edge of freedom of expression. During this period, the Foundation maintained its contacts and program activities with the government, one major focus of which was legislative development. It was well placed to move to a democracy promotion program in 1986 when the government signaled the beginning of a democratic transition with elections.[9]

14. Go light on "official" assistance but provide a mechanism for the appropriation of modest, low-profile funds.

One of the primary drawbacks of nongovernmental organizations, whatever their program focus or status in the host country, is their relatively small funding base. The long-term nature of the liberalization process requires a financial commitment that NGOs may find difficult to meet. It is in the U.S. interest to make government funds available for this purpose. However, it is frequently difficult to extract funds from the underbrush of legislative restrictions that apply to many authoritarian countries. Consideration of waivers or other mechanisms to provide funds on an individual case basis is often too politically inflammatory to be an effective strategy.

The annual congressional appropriations to American quasi-nongovernmental organizations, or QUANGOs, can be applied to support liberalization in these countries. However, current levels of QUANGO funding are too low for these organizations to respond to many opportunities. Beyond raising QUANGO appropriations, Congress should also consider establishing a separate and ongoing program with modest funds to promote openness in liberalizing countries. To do so would require a categorical legislative waiver to allow assistance to countries that are otherwise prohibited from receiving U.S. government funds for this specific purpose. This waiver should permit American NGOs to use economic support funds or developmental assistance appropriated through Foreign Operations bills to support governmental and civil society trends that contribute to liberalization. The waiver should require consultation between the administration and Congress on its use. These consultations would provide a more cooperative basis for discussion on methods of encouraging change in authoritarian countries than the high-profile (but rarely productive) debates that result from more ad hoc exercises.

15. Encourage international business to focus corporate philanthropy on support for liberalization.

One frequent criticism of the American business community in debates over human rights and democracy promotion policy is that its approach to "engagement" in authoritarian countries is entirely laissez-faire. Claims that commerce will lead automatically to economic growth in the host country, and automatically from there to greater freedom, are often regarded as specious because they require no effort or change on the part of business. Moreover, although history suggests that raising the economic levels of a population makes it more inclined to political openness and the protection of human rights, there is no firm timeline for this process. As the evidence in previous chapters suggests, market reform and the rapid development of a commercial sector can create opportunities for liberalization and eventual democratization by diminishing the size and control of the state and by giving new power to the media and other groups that stand to benefit from commercialization. But it can also be harmful to the prospects for democratization in the short and medium term by creating new economic oligarchies that are themselves antidemocratic, as well as by strengthening elements of the middle classes that are prone to putting self-interest over public interest. Although they cannot engineer the greater process of political change in authoritarian countries, external actors can help reinforce the benefits of market reform and commerce and can aid societies in addressing the drawbacks.

American business therefore needs to abandon its reliance on sanguine correlations and take a more proactive approach to promoting constructive political change. The philanthropy programs of international corporations that do business in liberalizing authoritarian countries are a potential, but largely untapped, source of funds for this purpose. These funds are not subject to the wide variety of restrictions placed upon official assistance. Within the United States, corporate donations are often applied to innovative social projects that are considered to be too experimental for government funding. However, the reverse is usually the case in their international programs. Corporations fear projects that may antagonize the host country government. Moreover, donations are often employed to serve an immediate public relations or marketing purpose rather than a long-term goal.

Corporations frequently stress the influence of their corporate ethics and business practices upon the host community, particularly in their treatment of local employees.[10] How tangible an effect this can have on the political and social fabric of a target country is open to debate, in part because of scale: most Chinese, for example, do not work for Beijing Jeep. Nevertheless, the efforts of American business in recent years to codify their best practices and to make their labor standards more transparent often have a positive effect.

These trends are strengthened by several models of business codes put forward by social activists (such as the Sullivan Principles for South Africa), the U.S. government (the Clinton administration's Model Business Principles of 1995), individual corporations (Levi Strauss's Business Partner Terms of Engagement) and coalitions of nongovernmental and business groups (the 1999 U.S. Business Principles for Human Rights of Workers in China).[11]

In their corporate philanthropy, U.S. multinational corporations can utilize sensible guidelines to support activities contributing to openness that parallel those of other groups working in this area. Projects that support host country government goals, such as legal development, or NGOs that provide social services (but avoid high-profile political positions) are obvious candidates. Corporations may further protect themselves through the use of go-betweens. Funds can be made available to American NGOs for project implementation under Section 501(c)(3) of the Internal Revenue Code and its regulations. Corporations may also contribute funds to umbrella projects, which can be organized by business councils or other intermediary organizations. One such noteworthy experiment is the U.S.-China Legal Cooperation Fund, established and managed by the United States-China Business Council. This program was intended to support the administration's Rule of Law Initiative arising from the 1997–98 U.S.-China summits but operates as a private effort.[12]

Shaping more effective and credible strategies for engagement with authoritarian states that are experimenting with openness should be the thrust of broader U.S. post–cold war policy as well. The polarization of policy debate toward these countries—indeed the paralysis of policy in many cases—can be attributed to the search for automatic mechanisms, be they ideology or economics. This study argues that such wishful thinking should be abandoned on both sides. Many of the tools to promote change in these countries are immediately at hand, if the results are not yet within grasp.

Notes

Chapter One

1. Radek Sikorski, "How We Lost Poland," *Foreign Affairs*, vol. 75 (September–October 1996), p. 15. See also Tina Rosenberg, "The Unfinished Revolution of 1989," *Foreign Policy*, no. 115 (Summer 1999), pp. 90–105; and Peter Rutland, "The Revolutions of 1989 Reconsidered," *Current History*, vol. 98 (April 1999), pp. 147–52.

2. A wealth of literature detailing these transitions has appeared in the past decade. However, the most useful single-volume analysis remains Samuel P. Huntington's *The Third Wave: Democratization in the Late Twentieth Century* (University of Oklahoma Press, 1991), even though it predates the transitions in the former Soviet Union and some African states.

3. Guillermo O'Donnell and Philippe Schmitter, *Transitions from Authoritarian Rule: Tentative Conclusions About Uncertain Democracies* (Johns Hopkins University Press, 1986), pp. 5–6. Much of the theoretical discussion in this chapter is informed by this work, one of the major studies of regime change in the 1980s.

4. This term was coined in the 1980s by Professor Robert Scalapino, University of California at Berkeley, to describe loosening systems in Asia on both ends of the political spectrum.

5. I am indebted to Professor James Feinerman of the Georgetown University Law Center for bringing this proverb to my attention.

6. Larry Diamond, *Developing Democracy: Toward Consolidation* (Johns Hopkins University Press, 1999), p. 261.

7. Ibid., p. 270.

8. For two thoughtful and opposing views of the present and future impact of political Islam, see John Esposito, "Claiming the Center: Political Islam in Transition," *Harvard International Review*, vol. 19 (Spring 1997), pp. 8–13; and Martin Kramer,

"Ballots and Bullets: Islamists and the Relentless Drive for Power," in the same issue, pp. 16–20. See also Stephen S. Rosenfeld, "Political Space for 'Political Islam,'" *Washington Post*, September 12, 1997.

9. For discussion of the potential effects of democratization on regional politics in the Middle East, see Jane Perlez, "A Middle East Choice: Peace or Democracy," *New York Times*, November 28, 1999.

10. For a brief comparison of political and economic reform in China and Vietnam, see Philip Bowring, "Vietnam Hasn't Stopped Reforms, but the Progress Is Slow," *International Herald Tribune*, December 2, 1999.

11. Some scholars have suggested that the catalyst for this shift will be the death of 90-year-old General Ne Win, who officially ruled Burma from 1962 to 1988 and is believed to have traded overt power for that of a political puppet-master. From this perspective, the present junta, the State Peace and Development Council, cannot be considered second-generation leadership. See David Steinberg and others, "Indonesia and Myanmar," in *Regional Outlook: Southeast Asia, 1999–2000* (Singapore: Institute for Southeast Asian Studies, 1998), pp. 20–33.

12. For a description of the uniform approach taken by the United States to supporting democracy in Eastern Europe after 1989, see Thomas Carothers, *Assessing Democracy Assistance: The Case of Romania* (Washington: Carnegie Endowment for International Peace, 1996).

13. Diamond, *Developing Democracy*, p. 216.

14. See Mark. R. Thompson, *The Anti-Marcos Struggle: Personalistic Rule and Democratic Transition in the Philippines* (Yale University Press, 1995); and Karl O. Jackson, "The Philippines: The Search for a Suitable Democratic Solution, 1946–86," in Larry Diamond, ed., *Democracy in Developing Countries: Asia* (Boulder, Colo.: Lynne Rienner, 1989), pp. 231–66.

15. This view is so pervasive it has become the object of caricature. For example, *New York Times* columnist Thomas Friedman chides Americans for their perception of China as "a big prison where everyone is making replicas of the Statue of Liberty in the basement." Thomas L. Friedman, "Seeing China in 3-D," *New York Times*, May 18, 1999.

16. See, for example, U.S. Department of State, *Strategic Plan for International Affairs* (1997); and U.S. Office of Management and Budget, *The Budget for Fiscal Year 2000* (1999).

17. For discussion of the undertow of the Third Wave, see Fareed Zakaria, "The Rise of Illiberal Democracy," *Foreign Affairs*, vol. 76 (November–December 1997), pp. 22–43; and Robert Kaplan, "Was Democracy Just a Moment?" *Atlantic Monthly*, vol. 280 (December 1997), pp. 55–80.

18. Jerry F. Hough, *Democratization and Revolution in the USSR, 1985–1991* (Brookings, 1997), p. 11.

19. Ibid., p. 10.

20. "A Poor Start for Putin," *International Herald Tribune*, May 16, 2000.

21. Adrian Karatnycky, "Nations in Transit: From Change to Permanence," in Adrian Karatnycky, Alexander Motyl, and Charles Graybow, eds., *Nations in Transit, 1998: Civil Society, Democracy, and Markets in East Central Europe and the Newly Independent States* (New Brunswick, N.J.: Transaction Publishers, 1999), pp. 12–13.

22. John M. Kramer, "The Politics of Corruption," *Current History*, vol. 97 (October, 1998), p. 331. See also Stephen Handelman, "Stealing the Dream: 'Bandit Capitalism' in the Post-Communist States," in Karatnycky, Motyl, and Graybow, eds., *Nations in Transit, 1998*, pp. 21–28.

23. Elizabeth Reisch, "Albright: Russia Is Not Ours to Lose," in *Carnegie Endowment for International Peace Russian and Eurasian Affairs Program Issue Brief*, vol. 1 (September 16, 1999), p. 1.

24. For an account of American attempts to promote political development in the early years of the cold war that goes far beyond its title, see Theodore P. Wright, *American Support of Free Elections Abroad* (Washington: Public Affairs Press, 1964).

25. See the classic study by Daniel Pipes and Adam Garfinkle, eds., *Friendly Tyrants: An American Dilemma* (St. Martin's Press, 1991).

26. See Thomas Carothers, *In the Name of Democracy: U.S. Policy Toward Latin America in the Reagan Years* (University of California Press, 1991).

27. For a discussion of the cold war origins of the Endowment, see Thomas Carothers, "The NED at 10," *Foreign Policy*, no. 95 (Summer 1994), p. 123.

28. See United States General Accounting Office, *Promoting Democracy: Foreign Affairs and Defense Agencies Funds and Activities—1991 to 1993*, GAO/NSLAD-94-83 (1994), p. 4.

29. These programs were authorized, and continue to be funded, under the Support for Eastern European Democracy Act of 1989 (Pub. L. 101–179, 103 Stat. 1298) and the Freedom Support Act of 1992 (Pub. L. 102-511, 106 Stat. 3320).

30. See United States Agency for International Development, *The Democracy Initiative* (December 1990). Although this initiative brought new democracy programs to some countries, in others it repackaged assistance that had been funded under Section 116(e) of the Foreign Assistance Act (codified as amended at 22 U. S. C. § 2151n[e]). However, in contrast to 116(e) projects, which tended to focus on short-term, single activities, assistance under the Democracy Initiative yielded more programs with three- to five-year time frames. This reflected not only a greater commitment to democracy assistance but also a more systematic approach. Moreover, Section 116(e) grants were often aimed at societies approaching a democratic transition, while the larger packages of the Democracy Initiative intended to address the multipronged problem of consolidating democracy.

31. Indicators are listed in the annual presentations submitted to Congress by the U.S. Agency for International Development in support of the administration's budget request for each fiscal year.

32. U.S. Agency for International Development, *The Democracy Initiative*, pp. 3–4.

33. For a critique of the sustainable development formula from another vantage point, that of economic development, see Michael O'Hanlon and Carol Graham, *A Half Penny on the Federal Dollar: The Future of Development Aid* (Brookings, 1997).

34. For an illuminating case study that examines the relationship between democratization and conflict resolution, see Terrence Lyons, *Voting for Peace: Post-Conflict Elections in Liberia* (Brookings, 1999).

35. For official use of this terminology and the essential architecture of this approach, see U.S. Agency for International Development, *Constituencies for Reform: Strategic Approaches for Donor-Supported Civil Advocacy Programs* (1995), pp. 4–5.

36. Iliya Harik, "Pluralism in the Arab World," *Journal of Democracy*, vol. 5 (July 1994), p. 48.

37. Robin Wright, "Letter from Teheran: We Invite the Hostages to Return," *New Yorker*, November 8, 1999, p. 39.

38. The bellwether phenomenon occasionally has played a role in normalizing relations. In the mid-1980s, prominent former Vietnam prisoners of war, such as Senator John McCain and Representative Douglas ("Pete") Peterson, were vocal in supporting normalization with Hanoi. Peterson subsequently became the first U.S. ambassador to Vietnam after 1975, and the first ever to Hanoi. More recently, Bruce Laingen, the highest-ranking U.S. official held hostage in Iran, has urged increased contact between Washington and Teheran. See, for example, Bruce Laingen, "It's Time for the U.S. and Iran to Sit Down and Talk," *Christian Science Monitor*, March 12, 1998.

39. See, for example, Thomas L. Friedman's "China's Nationalist Tide," *New York Times*, March 16, 1996.

40. Bay Fang, "Chinese Students are 'Feeling Their Oats,'" *U.S. News & World Report*, July 13, 1998.

41. Lucian Pye, "Political Science and the Crisis of Authoritarianism," *American Political Science Review*, vol. 84 (March 1990), p. 10.

42. Anthony M. Cordesman and Ahmed S. Hashim, *Iran: Dilemmas of Dual Containment* (Boulder, Colo.: Westview Press, 1997), pp. 45–46.

43. See remarks by Mark Gasiorowski and Suzanne Maloney at a Brookings Institution press briefing, "Elections in Iran: What Happened? Why? And Will It Matter?" Washington, February 23, 2000 (www.brook.edu/comm/transcripts/20000223.htm [June 2000]).

44. Emmanual Sivan, "Constraints and Opportunities in the Arab World," *Journal of Democracy*, vol. 8 (April 1997), pp. 103–13.

45. Diamond, *Developing Democracy*, p. 263.

46. See Gerald Segal, "From Indonesia: A Warning to Asian Authoritarians," *International Herald Tribune*, June 5, 1998.

47. For a discussion of the latter, see John Orme, "Dismounting the Tiger: Lessons from Four Liberalizations," *Political Science Quarterly*, vol. 103 (Summer 1988), pp. 245–65.

48. See, for example, Samuel Huntington and Clement H. Moore, eds., *Authoritarian Politics in Modern Society: The Dynamics of Established One-Party Systems* (Basic

Books, 1970); James M. Malloy, ed., *Authoritarianism and Corporatism in Latin America* (University of Pittsburgh Press, 1977); and Juan J. Linz, "Totalitarian and Authoritarian Regimes," in Fred I. Greenstein and Nelson W. Polsby, eds., *Handbook of Political Science*, vol. 3 (Addison-Wesley, 1975), pp. 175–412.

49. See Juan J. Linz, *The Breakdown of Democratic Regimes: Crisis, Breakdown, and Reequilibration* (Johns Hopkins University Press, 1978). The term *redemocratization* has re-emerged in post–cold war vocabularies in a different guise. Democratic transitions are often referred to as attempts to "return to democracy" or "restore democracy," even in countries with no prior democratic period.

50. Mark J. Gasiorowski, "The Political Regimes Project," in Alex Inkeles, ed., *On Measuring Democracy: Its Consequences and Concomitants* (New Brunswick, N.J.: Transaction Publishers, 1991), p. 110.

51. I thank Thomas Carothers, vice president for studies at the Carnegie Endowment for International Peace, for this observation.

52. William Watts, "Americans Look at Asia: An Analysis of a Public Opinion Survey," pp. 45–47 (www.hluce.org/survey.html [June 2000]). This survey was funded by the Henry Luce Foundation and presented at the foundation's October 19, 1999, symposium in Washington.

53. Gasiorowski, "The Political Regimes Project," p. 109.

54. The O'Donnell and Schmitter *Transitions from Authoritarian Rule* project takes precisely this approach. I am indebted to Dr. Marina Ottaway, senior associate at the Carnegie Endowment for International Peace, for pointing this out.

55. Mark J. Gasiorowski, "An Overview of the Political Regime Change Dataset," *Comparative Political Studies*, vol. 29 (August 1996), pp. 469–83.

56. Noteworthy works to date include Harry Harding, *China's Second Revolution: Reform After Mao* (Brookings, 1987); Kenneth Lieberthal, *Governing China: From Revolution through Reform* (Norton, 1995); and Andrew Nathan, *China's Transition* (Columbia University Press, 1997).

Chapter Two

1. Alexis de Tocqueville, *The Old Regime and the French Revolution* (Doubleday, 1955), p. 177.

2. For example, political scientist Joseph Fewsmith has said of Chinese president Jiang Zemin that he "seems to be willing to give people more liberal space, but gets very upset if they try to take it." Susan V. Lawrence, "Jiang's Two Faces," *Far Eastern Economic Review*, December 2, 1999, p. 17.

3. Bertil Lintner, "Two Steps Back," *Far Eastern Economic Review*, December 18, 1997, p. 32. For a more extensive discussion of the effects of the economic crisis on Vietnam, see William Turley, "Vietnam: Ordeals of Transition," in Karl D. Jackson, ed., *Asian Contagion: The Causes and Consequences of a Financial Crisis* (Boulder, Colo.: Westview Press, 1999), pp. 269–99.

4. For a thorough and objective analysis of this problem, see William B. Quandt, *Between Ballots and Bullets: Algeria's Transition from Authoritarianism* (Brookings, 1998).

5. U.S. Department of State, Bureau of Democracy, Human Rights and Labor, "Algeria Country Report on Human Rights Practices for 1998," *1998 Human Rights Report* (February 26, 1999), p. 1 (www.state.gov/www/global/human_rights/1998_hrp_report/algeria.html [June 2000]).

6. This "lingering extinction" theory did indeed work against the Khmer Rouge in Cambodia in the 1990s. After the Khmer Rouge refused to honor the Paris peace accords of 1991, the party was excluded from the new political and economic systems built largely with international assistance. By the late 1990s the death of revolutionary leader Pol Pot and defections of key Khmer Rouge leaders signaled the end of the Khmer Rouge as a political entity. See Catharin Dalpino, *Resolving the Cambodian Conflict: Lessons for the International Community* (New York: Asia Society, 1999).

7. Augustus Richard Norton, "Rethinking United States Policy toward the Muslim World," *Current History*, vol. 98 (February 1999), p. 55.

8. See Glenn E. Robinson, "Can Islamists Be Democrats? The Case of Jordan," *Middle East Journal*, vol. 51 (Summer 1997), pp. 373–87.

9. Ibid., p. 387.

10. Catharin Dalpino, "Human Rights in China," Brookings Policy Brief 50 (June 1999), p. 2.

11. A discussion of this period can be found in Jacques Bertrand, "False Starts, Succession Crises and Regime Transition: Flirting with Openness in Indonesia," *Pacific Affairs*, vol. 69 (Fall 1996), pp. 319–40. See also Adam Schwarz, *A Nation in Waiting: Indonesia in the 1990s* (Boulder, Colo.: Westview Press, 1994); and Michael R. J. Vatikiotis, *Indonesian Politics Under Suharto: Order, Development and Pressure for Change* (Routledge, 1993).

12. This is not meant to suggest a parallel between the rise of political Islam in the Middle East and the strengthening of Muslim groups in Indonesia. Southeast Asia subscribes to a different school of Islam than does the Middle East, and in Indonesia in particular, Islamic fundamentalism does not figure prominently in political life. The Muslim organizations that played a part in the political events of 1998 were largely "secular," that is, did not advocate the installation of an Islamic regime in Indonesia.

13. Gordon P. Means, "Soft Authoritarianism in Malaysia and Singapore," *Journal of Democracy*, vol. 7 (October 1996), p. 103–07.

14. In "Dismounting the Tiger: Lessons from Four Liberalizations" (*Political Science Quarterly*, vol. 103 [Summer 1988], pp. 245–65), John Orme considers both of these transitions at length. For additional discussion of Spain's transition, see U.S. Department of State, Bureau of Intelligence and Research, "Transitions from Authoritarianism: 'The Man in the Middle,'" Unclassified Intelligence Assessment (July 28, 1975).

15. James Cotton, "From Authoritarianism to Democracy in South Korea," *Political Studies*, vol. 37 (June 1989), p. 245.

16. The Taiwan model has been insufficiently studied in the literature on political change. However, useful works include Linda Chao and Ramon H. Meyers, *The First*

Chinese Democracy: Political Life in the Republic of China on Taiwan (Johns Hopkins University Press, 1998); Steven J. Hood, *The Kuomintang and the Democratization of Taiwan* (Boulder, Colo.: Westview, 1997); Hung-mao Tien, "The Transformation of an Authoritarian Party-State: Taiwan's Developmental Experience," *Issues and Studies*, vol. 25 (July 1989), pp. 125–29; and Kuo Tai-chun and Ramon H. Meyers, "The Great Transition: Political Change and the Prospects for Democracy in the Republic of China on Taiwan," *Asian Affairs*, vol. 15 (Fall 1998), pp. 115–33. In keeping with the focus of the 1990s, most studies emphasize the democratization process—whose beginnings were traced to the 1986–88 period, when martial law was lifted and opposition parties were allowed to operate—and give less attention to the liberalization era that commenced in the late 1970s.

17. Hung-mao Tien, "The Transformation of an Authoritarian Party-State," p. 123.

18. Kuo Tai-chun and Ramon Meyers, "The Great Transition," p. 117.

19. "Arabs Tiptoe to Democracy," *Economist*, August 7, 1999, pp. 33–34.

20. See "Iran Morality Tale," *Washington Post*, March 4, 1999.

21. A recent test case in China, which attracted considerable attention in the West, was the attempt to establish and register an opposition party, the Chinese Democratic Party, by a small group of dissidents. See "China: Don't Need a Weatherman," *Economist*, December 5, 1998, pp. 52–53; Fred Hiatt, "Where Democracy is a Crime," *Washington Post*, December 28, 1998; and Richard Cohen, "Scream at China," *Washington Post*, December 29, 1998.

22. This was the central thesis of the studies on Latin America by Guillermo O'Donnell and Philippe Schmitter, who interpret most decisions to liberalize as narrow power-struggles between regime leaders or factions, most often to reshuffle the hierarchy or settle issues of succession. In *The Third Wave: Democratization in the Late Twentieth Century* (University of Oklahoma Press, 1991), Samuel Huntington gives this view some credence, but he assigns equal weight to "external factors" such as social unrest or the consequences of economic change. There was evidence of both these dynamics in the Deng Xiaoping era in China. Some scholars attribute Deng's decision to reform in the late 1970s to internal regime maneuvering (repudiating the ideology of Mao Tse-tung, in order to establish a political base for himself), while others point to broader domestic factors (the need for economic recovery following the Cultural Revolution). For studies of the reform process in the Deng era and the interplay of these two factors, see Merle Goldman, *Sowing the Seeds of Democracy in China: Political Reform in the Deng Xiaoping Era* (Harvard University Press, 1994); and Carol Lee Hamrin and Suisheng Zhao, *Decision-Making in Deng's China: Perspectives from Insiders* (Armonk, N.Y.: M.E. Sharpe, 1995).

23. For elaboration on these categories, see Su Shaozhi, "Ideological Struggles in Contemporary China," *Freedom Review*, vol. 27 (September–December 1996), pp. 11–13.

24. See Dean Yates, "Vietnam's Leaders Do It Their Way," Reuters Wire Service, September 15, 1998.

25. Eric Hooglund, "Khatami's Iran," *Current History*, vol. 98 (February 1999), pp. 61–62.

26. Ibid., pp. 62–63.

27. See, for example, Saad Eddin Ibrahim, "Iran: The Return of the Moderates," *Civil Society*, vol. 6 (June 1997), p. 4; and Scott Macleod, "Passionate Politics," *Time*, April 27, 1998, p. 42.

28. Su Shaozhi, "Ideological Struggles in Contemporary China," pp. 19–20.

29. For example, some Western observers expressed disappointment with Khatami's muted response to the arrest of thirteen Iranian Jews in the summer of 1999. See Reuel Marc Gerecht, "More Mullah Than Moderate," *Washington Post*, July 8, 1999.

30. For a discussion of this problem with respect to China, see Allen C. Choate, "Building Trust in the United States-China Relationship," Asia Foundation Working Paper 4 (San Francisco, 1997), pp. 10–11.

31. For an elaboration of this point, see Minxin Pei, "Semi-Authoritarianism in China: Potential for Further Reform?" paper presented at *The Growing Challenges of Semi-Authoritarianism*, Carnegie Endowment for International Peace Study Group, Washington, D.C., December 2, 1998.

32. I am indebted to Mike Jendrzejcyk, Washington director of Human Rights Watch/Asia for this point.

33. Susan V. Lawrence, "Agent of Change," *Far Eastern Economic Review*, July 23, 1998, pp. 10–12. Lawrence notes that these party-initiated public debates in China are a significant departure from those in the 1980s. Then policy discussions were more hermetic, confined to top party insiders who used ideas as weapons in internal struggles.

34. Steve Mufson, "Technocrats' Hustle Helps Party Keep Up With Change," *Washington Post*, June 17, 1998. Minxin Pei goes so far as to see a "technocrat-dominated center within the ruling elite" in China, in "Microfoundations of State-Socialism and Patterns of Economic Transformation," *Communist and Post-Communist Studies*, vol. 29 (June 1996), p. 142.

35. Suisheng Zhao, "Political Reform and Changing One-Party Rule in Deng's China," *Problems of Post-Communism*, vol. 44 (September–October 1997), p. 18.

36. For a more extensive discussion of this era, see Catharin Dalpino, "Thailand's Search for Accountability," in Larry Diamond and Marc F. Plattner, eds., *The Global Resurgence of Democracy* (Johns Hopkins University Press, 1993), pp. 206–16.

37. U.S. Department of State, "Iran Country Report on Human Rights Practices for 1998," *1998 Human Rights Report* (1999), p. 5 (www.state.gov/www/global/human_rights/1998_hrp_report/iran.html [June 2000]).

38. "Tense Days in Tehran," *New York Times*, April 26, 2000.

39. For a discussion of the Consultative Council's composition and development, see R. Hrair Dekmejian, "Saudi Arabia's Consultative Council," *Middle East Journal*, vol. 52 (Spring 1998), pp. 204–18.

40. Daniel L. Byman and Jerrold D. Green, "The Enigma of Political Stability in the Persian Gulf Monarchies," *Middle East Review of International Affairs*, vol. 3 (September 1999), pp. 10–11.

41. Kevin J. O'Brien, "Chinese People's Congresses and Legislative Embeddedness," *Comparative Political Studies*, vol. 27 (April 1994), p. 82. O'Brien likens the present state of the National People's Congress in China to early English and European parliaments.

However, he disputes popular accounts of the development of those institutions and argues that strengthening them was a more cooperative venture with executive branches than a confrontational one.

42. Ibid., pp. 86–87.

43. Minxin Pei, "Democratization in the Greater China Region," *Access Asia Review*, vol. 1 (July 1998), pp. 31–32.

44. Hugh J. Ivory, "Leninist Parliaments and Reform: The Development of China's National People's Congress Since 1983," unpublished dissertation, University of London, 1995, p. 31.

45. Minxin Pei, "Democratization in the Greater China Region," p. 32.

46. Testimony of Lorne W. Craner, President of the International Republican Institute for International Affairs, in *U.S. Policy Options toward China: Rule of Law and Democracy Programs*, Hearings before the House International Relations Committee, Subcommittee on Asia and the Pacific, 105 Cong. 2 sess. (April 30, 1998), p. 3.

47. Minxin Pei, "Is China Democratizing?" *Foreign Affairs*, vol. 77 (January–February 1998), p. 76.

48. "China's Parliament in Waiting," *Economist*, November 2, 1996, p. 34.

49. Ivory, "Leninist Parliaments and Reform," p. 29.

50. Minxin Pei, "Creeping Democratization in China," *Journal of Democracy*, vol. 6 (October 1995), p. 71.

51. Gabriel Kolko, *Vietnam: Anatomy of a Peace* (Routledge, 1997), p. 131.

52. U.S. Department of State, "Vietnam Country Report on Human Rights Practices for 1997," *1997 Human Rights Report* (January 30, 1998), p. 10 (www.state.gov/www/global/human_rights/1997_hrp_report/vietnam.html [June 2000]).

53. Frederick Z. Brown, "Vietnam's Tentative Transformation," *Journal of Democracy*, vol. 7 (October 1996), p. 82.

54. Huw Watkin, "'Parliament TV' Opens MPs to Public Scorn," *South China Morning Post*, December 3, 1999.

55. Faith Keenan, "Vietnam: No Rubber Stamp," *Far Eastern Economic Review*, December 10, 1998, p. 26.

56. Howard Schneider, "Kuwait at Odds on Women's Rights Issues," *Washington Post*, December 5, 1999. See also Mary Ann Tetreault, "Women's Rights in Kuwait: Bringing in the Last Bedouins?" *Current History*, vol. 99 (January 2000), pp. 27–32.

57. "A Hundred Years of Fortitude," *Economist*, November 27, 1999, p. 43.

58. As the Thai system has become more democratic, new constitutions have focused on institutional reform rather than on providing legal cover for new dictatorships. See James R. Klein, "The Constitution of the Kingdom of Thailand, 1997: A Blueprint for Participatory Democracy," Asia Foundation Working Paper 8 (San Francisco, 1998).

59. I am grateful to Professor David Steinberg, director of Asian Studies, Edmund A. Walsh School of Foreign Service, Georgetown University, for this observation.

60. Shireen T. Hunter, "Is Iranian Perestroika Possible Without Fundamental Change?" *Washington Quarterly*, vol. 21 (Autumn 1998), p. 31.

61. For a discussion of the tension between these two traditions with respect to U.S.-China relations, see Robert A. Kapp, "China, the United States and the Rule of Law," *China Business Review*, November–December 1997, pp. 6–7. For a more general description of Western expectations for legal reform, see Thomas Carothers, "The Rule of Law Revival," *Foreign Affairs*, vol. 77 (March–April 1998), pp. 95–106.

62. Murray Scot Tanner, "Law in China: The *Terra Incognita* of Political Studies," *China Exchange News*, vol. 22 (Winter 1994), p. 21.

63. For an examination of this effect with respect to China, see Susan V. Lawrence, "China: Excising the Cancer," *Far Eastern Economic Review*, August 20, 1998, pp. 10–13; and Edward Cody, "China's New Wealth Fuels Crime Wave: Economic and Social Change Caused by Market Reforms Spurs Competition, Thievery," *Washington Post*, December 31, 1996.

64. For example, human rights groups maintain that the elimination of China's counter-revolutionary law in 1997 and corresponding revisions to the criminal code related to state security only serve to pour old wine into new bottles. See Human Rights Watch/ Asia, *China: Whose Security? State Security in China's New Criminal Code* (New York, 1997). For a more general discussion of reform of Chinese criminal law, see Lawyers Committee for Human Rights, *Opening to Reform? An Analysis of China's Revised Criminal Procedure Law* (New York, 1996). Vietnam also amended its security law in 1997 to give authorities broad powers to monitor citizens and to apply the penalty of "administrative detention," which confines an offender to a designated locality and government supervision. U.S. Department of State, "Vietnam Country Report on Human Rights Practices for 1998," *1998 Human Rights Report* (February 26, 1999), p. 3 (www.state.gov/www/global/ human_rights/1998_hrp_report/vietnam.html [June 2000]).

65. See, for example, Human Rights in China (HRIC) press release, "Bound and Gagged: Freedom of Association in China Further Curtailed Under New Regulations" (New York, November 13, 1998).

66. Jasper Becker, "Tightening the Noose on Parties," *South China Morning Post*, December 5, 1998.

67. Testimony of Allen C. Choate, director of Program Development, The Asia Foundation/Hong Kong in *U.S. Policy Options toward China*, Hearings before the House International Relations Committee, Subcommittee on Asia and the Pacific, 105 Cong. 2 sess. (April 30, 1998), pp. 4–5.

68. Minxin Pei, "Citizens vs. Mandarins: Administrative Litigation in China," *China Quarterly*, no. 152 (December 1997), p. 832.

69. Elisabeth Rosenthal, "Ordinary Chinese Are Suing the Powers That Be," *New York Times*, April 27, 1998. One of the most noteworthy (albeit fictional) anecdotes appears in a 1993 film by Chinese director Zhang Yimou, *The Story of Qui Ju*, which depicts the case of a peasant woman suing her village leader. The ironic resolution to the plot dramatizes the limitations and possibilities of Chinese legal reform at this time.

70. Bay Fang, "New Class Struggle," *Far Eastern Economic Review*, March 19, 1998, pp. 24–25.

71. Minxin Pei, "Democratization in the Greater China Region," p. 35.

72. See Allen C. Choate, "Legal Aid in China," Asia Foundation Working Paper 12 (San Francisco, 2000).

73. U.S. Department of State, "China Country Report on Human Rights Practices for 1997," *1997 Human Rights Report* (January 30, 1998) (www.state.gov/www/global/human_rights/1997_hrp_report/china.html [June 2000]). For a detailed analysis of the reform of neighborhood committees, see Allen C. Choate, "Local Governance in China, Part II: An Assessment of Urban Residents Committees and Municipal Community Development," Asia Foundation Working Paper 10 (San Francisco, 1998). Choate tracks the transformation of these institutions from agents of state control to providers of social services and community managers.

74. Stanley Karnow, *Vietnam: A History* (Viking Press, 1983), pp. 450–52.

75. Remarks of Mark Gasiorowski at Brookings Institution press briefing, "Elections in Iran: What Happened? Why? And Will It Matter?" Washington, February 23, 2000 (www.brook.edu/comm/transcripts/20000223.htm[June 2000]).

76. Although the phenomenon of Chinese village elections is widely noted in the West, the only book-length studies of this process to date have been published in China. Two of particular use to Western scholars were written by the China Rural Villagers Self-Government Research Group with funding from the Ford Foundation: *Study on the Election of Villagers Committees in Rural China* (Beijing: China Research Society of Basic-Level Government, 1993); and *Legal Systems of Village Committees in China* (Beijing: China Research Society of Basic-Level Government, 1995). Noteworthy articles and papers on this subject include Kevin J. O'Brien, "Implementing Political Reform in China's Villages," *Australian Journal of Chinese Affairs*, no. 32 (July 1994), pp. 33–59; Allen C. Choate, "Local Governance in China: An Assessment of Villagers Committees," Asia Foundation Working Paper 1 (San Francisco, 1997); Anne F. Thurston, "Muddling Toward Democracy: Political Change in Grassroots China," Peaceworks 23 (Washington: U.S. Institute of Peace, 1998); and Tianjian Shi, "Village Committee Elections in China: Institutional Tactics for Democracy," *World Politics*, vol. 51 (April 1999), pp. 385–412.

77. O'Brien, "Implementing Political Reform in China's Villages," pp. 40–41.

78. Thurston, "Muddling Toward Democracy," pp. iv–v.

79. U.S. Department of State, "Vietnam Country Report on Human Rights Practices for 1997," p. 5.

80. U.S. Department of State, "Laos Country Report on Human Rights Practices for 1997" (January 30, 1998), p. 5 (www.state.gov/www/global/human_rights/1997_hrp_report/laos.html [June 2000]).

81. "A Hundred Years of Fortitude," p. 43.

Chapter Three

1. Lester M. Salamon, "The Rise of the Nonprofit Sector," *Foreign Affairs*, vol. 73 (July–August 1994), pp. 109–10. The theoretical underpinnings of the introductory section of this chapter are informed by this article.

2. Mark Sidel, "The Emergence of a Nonprofit Sector and Philanthropy in the Socialist Republic of Vietnam," in Tadashi Tamamoto, ed., *Emerging Civil Society in the Asia Pacific Community* (Tokyo: Institute of Southeast Asian Studies and the Japan Center for International Exchange, 1996), p. 294.

3. For an account of the history and impact of intellectual movements in China, see Merle Goldman, "Politically Engaged Intellectuals in the 1990s," *China Quarterly*, no. 159 (September 1999), pp. 700–11.

4. For example, the President's Task Force on U.S. Government International Broadcasting characterized the populations under Asian authoritarian rule as "attempting to claw their way of out economic and political bondage." "Report of the President's Task Force on U.S. Government International Broadcasting," Department of State Publication 9925 (1991), p. 7.

5. Thomas P. Bernstein, "China: Change in a Marxist-Leninist State," in James W. Morley, ed., *Driven by Growth: Political Change in the Asia-Pacific Region* (Armonk, New York: M.E. Sharpe, 1993), p. 43.

6. Tony Saich, "The Search for Civil Society and Democracy in China," *Current History*, vol. 93 (September 1994), p. 263.

7. Barnett Baron, "Funding Civil Society in Asia: Philanthropy and Public-Private Partnerships," Asia Foundation Working Paper 3 (San Francisco, 1997), p. 28.

8. Barnett L. McCormick, Su Shaozhi, and Xiao Xiaoming, "The 1989 Democracy Movement: A Review of the Prospects for Civil Society in China," *Pacific Affairs*, vol. 65 (Summer 1992), p. 192.

9. Bernstein, "Change in a Marxist-Leninist State," p. 35.

10. Chai-anan Samudavanija, Kusuma Snitwongse, and Suchit Bunbungkorn, *From Armed Suppression to Political Offensive* (Bangkok: Institute of Security and International Studies, 1990), pp. 80–85.

11. David Steinberg, "The Road to Political Recovery: The Salience of Politics in Economics," in Robert I. Rotberg, ed., *Burma: Prospects for a Democratic Future* (Brookings, 1998), pp. 275–76.

12. I am indebted to Professor Wan Exiang of Wuhan University for this point.

13. Studies have shown this to be the case in democratizing as well as authoritarian states. See, for example, David G. Timberman, ed., *The Politics of Economic Reform in Southeast Asia: The Experiences of Thailand, Indonesia and the Philippines* (Manila: Asian Institute of Management, 1992). For a discussion of the impact of the shrinking state on systems undergoing simultaneous economic and political liberalization, see Christopher Young, "The Strategy of Political Liberalization: A Comparative View of Gorbachev's Reforms," *World Politics*, vol. 45 (October 1992), p. 47.

14. Linda Wong, "Privatization of Social Welfare in Post-Mao China," *Asian Survey*, vol. 34 (April 1994), pp. 320–21.

15. There is a growing body of literature on the development of civil society in China. Notable examples are Gordon White, Jude Howell, and Shang Xiaoyuan, *In Search of Civil Society: Market Reform and Social Change in Contemporary China* (Clarendon Press, 1996); Shu-yun Ma, "The Chinese Discourse on Civil Society," *China Quar-*

terly, no. 137 (March 1994), pp. 180–93; X.L. Ding, "Institutional Amphibiousness and the Transition from Communism: The Case of China," *British Journal of Political Science*, vol. 24 (July 1994), pp. 293–318; and Thomas Gold, "Party-State versus Society in China," in Joyce K. Kallgren, ed., *Building a Nation-State: China After Forty Years* (Berkeley: Center for Chinese Studies, 1990), pp. 125–51.

16. Matt Forney, "Voice of the People," *Far Eastern Economic Review*, May 7, 1998, pp. 10–12.

17. Pamela Yatsko, "Helping Hands," *Far Eastern Economic Review*, May 7, 1998, p. 14.

18. Henry S. Rowen, "The Short March: China's Road to Democracy," *National Interest*, no. 45 (Fall 1996), pp. 65–66.

19. Joseph Fewsmith, review of *Jiaofeng Sanci Sixiang Jiefang Shilu* (Crossed swords: A true account of the three periods of ideological liberation), in *Foreign Policy*, no. 113 (Winter 1998–99), pp. 109–10.

20. Rowen, "The Short March," p. 66.

21. Bay Fang, "Colorful Crusaders," *Far Eastern Economic Review*, May 7, 1998, p. 13.

22. Susan V. Lawrence, "Out of Bounds," *Far Eastern Economic Review*, December 24, 1998, p. 20.

23. Rowen, "The Short March," p. 66.

24. Orville Schell, "To Get Rich Is Glorious," *New Yorker,* July 25, 1994, p. 32.

25. Afshin Molavi, "Foreign Journal: Extra! Extra! Extra! Iran's Newspapers at War," *Washington Post*, August 30, 1999.

26. In this section, the term *NGOs* is used to denote the full range of civil society organizations found in liberalizing authoritarian states, although few if any would meet the criteria for NGOs in Western societies. This spectrum runs from GONGOs to groups that are completely self-paying. It is assumed, however, that all NGOs are subject to some degree of official control.

27. Sherry R. Lowrance, "After Beijing: Political Liberalization and the Women's Movement in Jordan," *Middle Eastern Studies*, vol. 34 (July 1998), pp. 83–94.

28. Mary Ann Tetreault, "Women's Rights in Kuwait: Bringing in the Last Bedouins?" *Current History*, vol. 99 (January 2000), p. 30.

29. "Top Rightist Is Picked to Head Powerful Iran Foundation," *International Herald Tribune*, July 23, 1999.

30. I am indebted to Suzanne Maloney, research associate in Foreign Policy Studies at the Brookings Institution, for most of the information contained in this paragraph.

31. I thank Suzanne Maloney for pointing this out.

32. John Cook and others, *The Rise of Non-Governmental Organizations in China: Implications for Americans* (New York: National Committee on U.S.-China Relations, 1994), p. 9.

33. Zhang Ye, "The Nature and Role of the Nongovernmental Sector in China," in *A Changing Asia: Women in Emerging Society*, Asian Perspective Series (San Francisco, Asia Foundation, 1998), p. 3.

34. Ibid. Zhang Ye gives the example of the All China Women's Federation as a long-standing mass organization that is taking on some of the characteristics of an NGO.

35. Salamon, "The Rise of the Nonprofit Sector," p. 120.

36. For an explication of regulations governing American NGOs that is intelligible to the nonlawyer and nonaccountant, see Russy D. Sumariwalla, "Charities and Non-profits in the U.S.: Regulation, Standard-Setting, Accreditation and Monitoring," Asia Foundation Working Paper 6 (San Francisco, 1998).

37. Quasi-nongovernmental organizations have been in existence in the United States since the early 1950s, but there is surprisingly little scholarship on them. The term was apparently coined in 1967 by Alan Pifer, then-president of the Carnegie Corporation, in an essay he wrote for the 1967 Carnegie Corporation Annual Report. Although outdated, the article is useful for its account of the establishment of QUANGOs in the context of cold war policy, as well as the advantages and incongruities of this model. I thank Christopher Sigur, executive director of the Japan Society of Northern California, for bringing this essay to my attention.

38. Hung-mao Tien, "The Transformation of an Authoritarian Party-State: Taiwan's Developmental Experience," *Issues and Studies*, vol. 25 (July 1989), pp. 125-29.

39. For an account of the liberalization period in South Africa, see Timothy Sisk, *Democratization in South Africa: The Elusive Social Contract* (Princeton University Press, 1995).

40. Forney, "Voice of the People," p. 12.

41. See, for example, Abraham S. Eisenstadt, ed., *Reconsidering Tocqueville's Democracy in America* (Rutgers University Press, 1988); Robert D. Putnam, with Robert Leonardi and Rafaella Nanetti, *Making Democracy Work: Civic Traditions in Modern Italy* (Princeton University Press, 1993); E. J. Dionne Jr., ed., *Community Works: The Revival of Civil Society in America* (Brookings, 1998); and Keith E. Whittington, "Revisiting Tocqueville's America," *American Behavioral Scientist*, vol. 42 (September 1998), pp. 21-32.

42. See Rex Brynen, Bahgat Korany, and Paul Noble, eds., *Political Liberalization and Democratization in the Arab World* (Boulder, Colo.: Lynne Rienner, 1995); and Augustus Richard Norton, ed., *Civil Society in the Middle East* (New York: E.J. Brill, 1995).

43. Mark R. Thompson, *The Anti-Marcos Struggle: Personalistic Rule and Democratic Transition in the Philippines* (Yale University Press, 1995), pp. 126-27.

44. The literature on this phenomenon is growing rapidly. Recent works include Jackie Smith, Charles Chatfield, and Ron Pagnucco, eds., *Transnational Social Movements and Global Politics: Solidarity Beyond the State* (Syracuse University Press, 1997); Donatella della Porta, Hanspeter Kriesi, and Dieter Rucht, eds., *Social Movements in a Globalizing World* (Macmillan, 1999); Jessica Matthews, "Power Shift: The Age of Nonstate Actors," *Foreign Affairs*, vol. 76 (January–February 1997), pp. 50–56; P. J. Simmons, "Learning to Live with NGO's," *Foreign Policy*, no. 112 (Fall 1998), pp. 82–84; and Jackie Smith, "Global Civil Society?" *American Behavioral Scientist*, vol. 42 (September 1998), pp. 93–107.

45. Matthews, "Power Shift," p. 55.

46. The NGOs' position in Vienna was presaged by a regional preparatory conference of Asian governments and NGOs in which these divergent positions emerged. See *Bangkok NGO Declaration of Human Rights* (Manila: Philippine Alliance of Human Rights, 1993).

47. Zhang Ye, "The Nature and Role of the Nongovernmental Sector in China," p. 5.

48. For an assessment of the impact of communications technology on globalization, see Robert O. Keohane and Joseph S. Nye Jr., "Power and Interdependence in the Information Age," *Foreign Affairs*, vol. 77 (September–October 1998), pp. 81–94.

49. Ibid., p. 81.

50. Zixiang Tan, Milton Mueller, and Will Foster, "China's New Internet Regulations: Two Steps Forward, One Step Back," *Communications of the Association for Computing Machinery,* vol. 40 (December 1997), p. 11.

51. Michael Laris, "Internet Police on the Prowl in China: Free Flow of Ideas Worries Leaders," *Washington Post*, October 24, 1998.

52. Mark Landler, "An Internet Vision in Millions," *New York Times*, December 23, 1999.

53. "China: The Great Wall Wired," *Economist*, February 7, 1998, p. 42. See also Joshua Cooper Ramo, "China Gets Wired," *Time*, May 11, 1998, pp. 52–54.

54. "China: Chinese Tunnel Through the Net," *Economist*, February 7, 1998, p. 43.

55. Grey E. Burkhart and Seymour E. Goodman, "The Internet Gains Acceptance in the Persian Gulf," *Communications of the Association for Computing Machinery*, vol. 41 (March 1998), pp. 19–22. See also Jon B. Alterman, "The Middle East's Information Revolution," *Current History*, vol. 99 (January 2000), pp. 21–26.

Chapter Four

1. Although this group was bipartisan, conservatives from the administration of President Ronald Reagan were quick to claim paternity for the cold war's end. Daniel Deudney and G. John Ikenberry describe this as the "Reagan victory school," which holds that Reagan's military and ideological assertiveness in the 1980s played the lead role in the collapse of Soviet communism. See Daniel Deudney and G. John Ikenberry, "Who Won the Cold War?" *Foreign Policy*, no. 87 (Summer 1992), pp. 123–37.

2. Bruce Parrott, "Democratization and Authoritarianism in Postcommunist Societies: Report of a Collaborative Study of Twenty-Seven Countries," State Department Research Contract 1724-447506 (Washington, 1997), p. 18.

3. Deudney and Ikenberry, "Who Won the Cold War?" pp. 134–35.

4. Ibid., p. 123.

5. See, for example, Jim Hoagland, ". . . So Little Knowledge," *Washington Post*, June 28, 1998.

6. See Conference Report on H.R. 4328, Making Omnibus Consolidated and Emergency Supplemental Appropriations for Fiscal Year 1999, 105 Cong. 2 sess., 144 Cong. Rec. H11085 (October 19, 1998). This is admittedly a difficult call, since the National League for Democracy (NLD) did win the 1990 national election, which the military set aside. To further complicate this issue, the Burmese opposition is located both in-country (comprising Aung San Suu Kyi and those NLD members who are out of prison at any given time) and on the Thai-Burmese border (student groups that fled Rangoon in 1988

and took refuge in the Karen ethnic stronghold). In principle, U.S. assistance aims to support both these opposition forces, but the difficulty of making in-country grants in Burma at this time means that the overwhelming proportion of funds goes to border groups.

7. Li Lu, "On Repression and Reform," *Journal of International Affairs*, vol. 49 (Winter 1996), p. 362.

8. This realpolitik coalition of strange bedfellows included the royalist National United Front for an Independent, Neutral, Peaceful, and Cooperative Cambodia (FUNCINPEC); the Khmer People's National Liberation Front (KPNLF), a remnant of the Long Nol regime that coalesced into a political party only after fleeing Cambodia; and the Khmer Rouge. The United States gave political support to the coalition as a whole, which held Cambodia's seat at the United Nations. U.S. financial support to the low-level military insurgency effort was confined to FUNCINPEC and KPNLF troops, and funds for Khmer Rouge forces were expressly prohibited.

9. See Foreign Operations, Export Financing, and Related Programs Appropriations Acts for fiscal years 1996 (H.R. 2863), 1997 (H.R. 3540), 1998 (H.R. 2159), and 1999 (H.R. 3196).

10. For example, the 1996 Annual Report of the National Endowment for Democracy describes a Burma grant for "a periodical published by exiled journalists and editors and smuggled into the country." National Endowment for Democracy, *Annual Report* (Washington, 1997), p. 16.

11. Testimony of Louisa Coan, senior program officer for Asia, National Endowment for Democracy, *U.S. Democracy Promotion in Asia*, Hearings before the Subcommittee on Asia and the Pacific, House International Relations Committee, 105 Cong. 1 sess. (September 17, 1997), p. 13.

12. Madelyn C. Ross and Kyna Rubin, "Changing China from Afar: Challenges for China's Activists in America," *Washington Journal of Modern China*, vol. 2 (Spring 1994), p. 34.

13. John Pomfret, "Dissidents Back China's WTO Entry," *Washington Post*, May 11, 2000.

14. Shu-yun Ma, "The Chinese Discourse on Civil Society," *China Quarterly*, no. 137 (March 1994), p. 185.

15. Ross and Rubin, "Changing China from Afar," p. 48. See also Carl Goldstein, "Innocents Abroad," *Far Eastern Economic Review*, September 15, 1994, pp. 22–24.

16. For example, the Chinese exile dissident community is split between veterans of the 1979 Democracy Wall movement and demonstrators in the 1989 Tiananmen Square movement. Ross and Rubin, "Changing China from Afar," pp. 38–39. For a description of tensions between Tiananmen Square leaders who fled and those who remained in China, see Chai Ling and others, "Tiananmen and the Future of China: The View Five Years Later," *Current History*, vol. 93 (September 1994), pp. 241–46.

17. "Report of the President's Task Force on U.S. Government International Broadcasting," Department of State Publication 9925 (1991), pp. 5–6.

18. Eduardo Lachica, "U.S. vs. China War of Words Continues Over the Airwaves," *Wall Street Journal*, September 27, 1996.

19. Bertil Lintner, "Heavy Static: Washington's Radio Free Asia Runs Into Trouble," *Far Eastern Economic Review*, March 24, 1994, p. 26.

20. Kenneth Katzman, *Iran: Current Developments and U.S. Policy*, CRS Issue Brief 93033 (Washington: Congressional Research Service, 1997), p. 15. Although Radio Free Iran is commonly (and more diplomatically) now referred to as "RFE's Persian service," Congress was unbending in the authorizing legislation and its official title remains Radio Free Iran.

21. "Review and Outlook: Radio Free Asia," *Wall Street Journal*, December 5, 1996.

22. Testimony of Richard Richter, president, Radio Free Asia, in *U.S. Democracy Promotion Programs in Asia,* Hearings before the Subcommittee on Asia and the Pacific, House International Relations Committee, 105 Cong., 1 sess.(September 17, 1999), p. 2.

23. Ibid.

24. Ibid.

25. Jack Donnelly, *International Human Rights* (Boulder, Colo.: Westview, 1993), p. 93. See also Neil J. Kritz, "The CSCE in the New Era," *Journal of Democracy*, vol. 4 (July 1993), pp. 17–28.

26. Donnelly, *International Human Rights*, pp. 95–96.

27. See Gareth Evans, "What Asia Needs Is a Europe-Style CSCA," *International Herald Tribune*, July 27, 1990.

28. The possible exception to this is the Asia-Pacific Economic Cooperation (APEC) group. However, although human rights issues are occasionally discussed on the margins of APEC, as East Timor was at the 1999 summit, there is no enthusiasm for inserting human rights into the APEC framework formally. Better possibilities for developing a human rights regime for Asia can be found at the subregional level, in Southeast Asia. In the mid-1990s, for example, the Human Rights Working Group of the Association of Southeast Asian Nations (ASEAN) was established with the eventual goal of crafting an ASEAN human rights code. This would have an obvious impact on Vietnam, Laos, and Burma but no direct bearing upon China. Given regional dynamics, it is doubtful than an ASEAN human rights framework would cross easily into Northeast Asia.

29. David I. Steinberg, "Talk to Burma's Generals," *Far Eastern Economic Review*, September 16, 1999, p. 32.

30. See, for example, the fiscal year 1996 bill for Foreign Operations, which required the Secretary of State to examine the feasibility of an Asian CSCE. Although the initiative called for mechanisms to monitor human rights protection in all the Pacific Rim states, it was ominously listed under the "China" subheading of the report. H.R. Rep.104-143, 104 Cong. 2 sess., p. 54. See also H.R. 2358 (the Political Freedom in China Act of 1997), 105 Cong. 1 sess., as passed by House of Representatives, November 5, 1997, Section 7 (143 Cong. Rec. H10063–64), proposing a "sense of Congress" that the United States should work actively to establish a CSCE in Asia. Similar proposals to address human rights in China have been included in drafts of other omnibus bills.

31. See Catharin Dalpino, "A Better Way to Persuade China," *Washington Post*, December 18, 1997.

32. Donnelly, *International Human Rights*, p. 93.

33. Executive Order 12850, "Conditions for Renewal of Most Favored Nation Status for the People's Republic of China in 1994" (May 28, 1993).

34. Donnelly, *International Human Rights*, pp. 122–23.

35. See, for example, Jonathan Mirsky, "China Plays the Dissident Card," *International Herald Tribune*, February 12, 1998; Matt Forney, "Pawn in the Game," *Far Eastern Economic Review*, April 20, 1998, pp. 24–25; and Todd Crowell and Paul Mooney, "Exporting Dissent," *Asiaweek*, May 1, 1998, p. 20.

36. Robert S. Ross, "China," in Richard N. Haass, ed., *Economic Sanctions and American Diplomacy* (New York: Council on Foreign Relations Press, 1998), pp. 20–21.

37. George Black, "Lower the Decibel Level on Human Rights," *Los Angeles Times*, March 10, 1997.

38. See, for example, Joan Nelson and Stephanie J. Eglinton, *Encouraging Democracy: What Role for Conditioned Aid?* (Washington: Overseas Development Council, 1992).

39. Richard N. Haass, "Conclusion: Lessons and Recommendations," in Haass, ed., *Economic Sanctions and American Diplomacy*, p. 203.

40. See European Commission Fact Sheet, "Proposed EU-China Village Governance Cooperation" (Brussels, 1998).

41. See Catharin Dalpino and Christopher Sigur, "Japan Can Help to Save Asia," *Washington Times*, March 13, 1998.

Chapter Five

1. See Jacques Bertrand, "False Starts, Succession Crises and Regime Transition: Flirting with Openness in Indonesia," *Pacific Affairs*, vol. 69 (Fall 1996), pp. 319–40, as well as Gordon Hein, "Indonesia in 1989: A Question of Openness," *Asian Survey*, vol. 30 (February 1990), p. 223.

2. As quoted in Felix Lo, "U.S. Academic Hails Clinton's China Trip," *China Daily*, May 29, 1998.

3. Remarks by Mark Gasiorowski at Brookings Institution press briefing, "Elections in Iran: What Happened? Why? And Will It Matter?" Washington, February 23, 2000 (www.brook.edu/comm/transcripts/20000223.htm[June 2000]).

4. Jack Bresnan, "A Case Study of Indonesia," in David G. Brown, ed., *Special Report—Southeast Asia: One Year After the Outbreak of the Financial Crisis, and Policy Implementation for the United States* (Washington: Woodrow Wilson International Center for Scholars, 1998), p. 16.

5. Jack Donnelly, *International Human Rights* (Boulder, Colo.: Westview, 1993), pp. 146–47.

6. For example, from 1995 through 1998 the administration attempted to persuade Congress to fund a modest program to support civil society in China, without success. One of the primary objections cited by members of Congress and their staffs was the lack of any truly independent nongovernmental organizations in the country.

Author's interviews with staff of the House Subcommittee on International Operations and Human Rights of the House International Relations Committee, 1996–98. See also U.S. Office of Management and Budget, *Budget for Fiscal Year 1997*, as well as budgets for fiscal 1998 and 1999.

7. American political sentiments frequently run counter to this principle. It is more common to permit the expenditure of funds for nongovernmental organizations in an authoritarian country but to forbid any funds for the government. For example, Section 526 of the fiscal 2000 Foreign Operations Bill (H.R. 2606) permits the expenditure of Economic Support Funds for nongovernmental organizations outside China to support "democracy-building activities" in China and expressly forbids assistance to the government.

8. As quoted in Brad Roberts, *Securing Democratic Transitions: Report of the Fourth Annual CSIS International Leadership Forum* (Washington: Center for Strategic and International Studies, 1990), p. 35.

9. See the annual reports (in some years titled *The President's Review*) of the Asia Foundation for the years 1977 to 1987 (San Francisco: Asia Foundation).

10. See Kevin T. Jackson, "Globalizing Corporate Ethics Programs: Perils and Prospects," *Journal of Business Ethics*, vol. 16 (September 1997), pp. 1227–35.

11. For further information on China-specific business codes, see Michael A. Santoro, *Profits and Principles: Global Capitalism and Human Rights in China* (Cornell University Press, 2000).

12. See United States-China Business Council press release, "U.S. Business Pledges Support for U.S.-China Rule of Law Cooperation," Washington, June 2, 1998.

Index

Africa, 18, 28, 65, 69, 85, 108
Algeria, 26, 27
All China Women's Federation, 121 n. 34
Anti-Rightist Campaign (China), 27
Apartheid, 65
APEC. *See* Asian-Pacific Economic
  Cooperation
Aquino, Corazon, 8
Arab-Israeli peace process, 5, 16
Arab Organization for Human Rights, 87
Argentina, 55
Aristide, Jean-Bertrand, 78
ASEAN. *See* Association of Southeast
  Asian Nations
Asia Foundation, The, 105
Asia-Pacific Economic Cooperation
  (APEC), 125 n. 28
Asian states, financial crisis, 25–26, 28
Asia-Pacific Forum of National Human
  Rights Institutions, 85–86
Association of Southeast Asian Nations
  (ASEAN), 86–87, 101, 125 n. 29
Aung San Suu Kyi, 123 n. 6
Australia, 85–86

Authoritarian systems: character of, 33;
  civil society in, 53–54, 55, 64, 67,
  68, 72; communications with, 69–72;
  definitions of, 23; demonstration effect,
  102; domino effect, 12–13; economic
  issues, 19–20; elections, 47–51; human
  rights, 85, 89, 99; international issues,
  67, 68; Internet use, 71–72; "intransigent" holdouts, 15–21; legal issues, 47;
  legislatures, 37–38; Leninist systems, 5;
  liberalization, 3–5, 7, 22, 25–51, 94;
  moderates, 30–35; nongovernmental
  organizations, 53, 61–62, 63, 64, 102,
  104; policy recommendations, 92–108;
  political opposition, 52–53; pressure for
  democracy, 9, 15, 20, 54; reforms, 25,
  30, 32, 44, 46–47, 72; ruling elites, 15;
  sanctions, 87–91; U.S. response to,
  73–91; Western democracies and, 32,
  51, 53, 54; women's rights, 50. *See also*
  Liberalization; individual countries

Bahrain, 37
Bangladesh, 48–49